MW01254224

Salisbury

Newburyport

Rowley
Ipswich
Essex
Danvers:
Beverly
Peabody
Marblehead
Salem
Lynn
Saugus
Nahant
Revere
Boston

Rockport

Gloucester

Manchester

Cape Ann

Massachusetts Bay

Atlantic Ocean

North Shore Lore

STORIES OF THE MASSACHUSETTS COAST

Ted Clarke

MASSACHUSETTS

Cape Cod Bay

4880 Lower Valley Road • Atglen, PA 19310

Schiffer Books are available at special discounts for bulk purchases for sales promotions or premiums. Special editions, including personalized covers, corporate imprints, and excerpts can be created in large quantities for special needs. For more information contact the publisher:

Published by Schiffer Publishing, Ltd.
4880 Lower Valley Road
Atglen, PA 19310
Phone: (610) 593-1777; Fax: (610) 593-2002
E-mail: Info@schifferbooks.com

For the largest selection of fine reference books on this and related subjects, please visit our website at **www.schifferbooks.com**
We are always looking for people to write books on new and related subjects. If you have an idea for a book, please contact us at proposals@schifferbooks.com

This book may be purchased from the publisher.
Please try your bookstore first.
You may write for a free catalog.

Designed by RoS
Type set in Elphinstone™/Adobe Caslon Pro

ISBN: 978-0-7643-4506-7
Printed in The United States of America

Photo Credits
Images are from the author's collection unless otherwise noted.
Cover image by Library of Congress

Other Schiffer Books By The Author:
The Charles River: A History of Greater Boston's Waterway
978-0-7643-4154-0 $24.99

Dedication

To my wife Mary,
for her patience and encouragement
during this lengthy process.

Contents

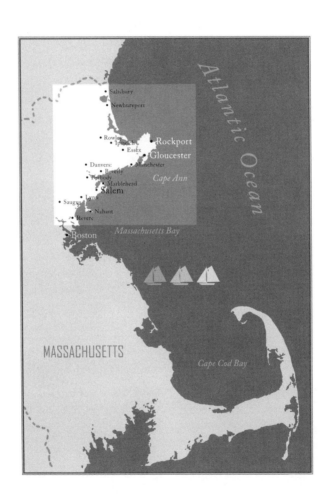

Atlantic Ocean

• Salisbury

• Newburyport

• Rowley
• Ipswich
• Essex

Rockport

Gloucester

• Danvers
• Beverly
• Peabody
• Marblehead

Salem

Cape Ann

• Manchester

• Lynn

• Saugus

• Nahant

• Revere

• Boston

Massachusetts Bay

MASSACHUSETTS

Cape Cod Bay

Introduction
The North Shore

The "North Shore" is not the official name of any geographic area. But it is used to describe some, or all, of the region northeast of Boston and south of the New Hampshire/Massachusetts border. To some it means only the coastal towns, or just the eastern part of Essex County, or the towns between Boston and Cape Ann. Here and there, towns that lie inland but are contiguous to coastal towns are addressed because they are economically or culturally similar to the coastal towns. I've written about all the coastal communities, including Winthrop and East Boston, which aren't usually thought of as North Shore, but do comprise the gateway to the region from Boston.

Living in Boston, or close to it, all my life, I'm familiar with the towns in this book—some more than others. During World War Two when most families didn't have cars to use, we traveled by public transportation to the easily accessible Revere Beach during its heyday, and sometimes to Lynn as well. As a teen, I often visited beaches like Marblehead and Crane's. Plum Island, Rockport, Gloucester, and Salem had many draws as well.

While many think of the region as one of wealthy suburbs with summer homes, estates, and quaint fishing villages, there are also working class towns, some of them with rundown sections. The area also has a lot of history to go with its interesting geography, and these make it a tourist attraction.

We've used most of the space in this book to write about the "lore"—the stories that make the North Shore interesting—or just interesting stories that belong to the North Shore. Some of these will be new to readers, or they will have been told in a different way than they've heard before. Since this "lore" is mostly history, and the "story" part is what makes history worthwhile, we'll use the narratives to bring life to the facts and events, and to relate them where possible to other facts and events. You won't have to study anything, but you may learn things anyway. These will be things you can readily remember, things you can then tell your friends, and perhaps the telling will make your conversation more interesting, too.

⚓

The Cape Ann Earthquake

Two hundred miles east of Boston, deep in the Atlantic, the captain of a merchant ship awoke with a start on November 18, 1855, when a loud thump alerted him to danger. Aroused from his deep-sea dream, he believed that his ship had hit a reef, a rock, or a sandbar. But that seemed unlikely 200 miles from shore, so he scrambled out on deck, where all was calm. He found the ocean current rippling, but silent; the dawn was spreading fingers of pink into the blackness of the eastern sky behind him, and his ship bobbed gently atop the waves.

More steady now himself, he dropped a sounding device over the port side and watched it descend. His instrument told him that his vessel was sailing in over 300 feet of deep sea water. There was no land in sight, no rocks, no reef. His ship could not have hit anything with its hull. Those things could not have caused the rousing thump which had roused him from his deep sleep.

What then had happened? He would have the answer only when he made port in Boston, early the next day. On the docks at Boston he learned that the resounding thud he had felt had been caused by an earthquake whose epicenter was at sea, not many miles from where he drifted during the early dawn and only twenty-five miles east of Rockport on Cape Ann. He had sailed over this epicenter of the quake as he completed his voyage to Boston. He, his ship, and its cargo were unharmed. But that could not be said of some places on land, including the North Shore.

The mysterious disturbance would be known as the "Cape Ann Earthquake of 1755," and it had a partner known widely as the "Great Earthquake of 1755," which had struck Lisbon, Portugal, just seventeen days earlier on November 1st. The Lisbon quake was one of the deadliest the world would ever know and the Cape Ann quake was the worst ever to strike New England—before or since.

The Cape Ann quake was felt as far north as Halifax, Nova Scotia, and south as far as South Carolina. Chimneys—a favorite target of this seismic event—were toppled in Portland, Springfield, and New Haven. Stone walls were wrecked throughout the region. Buildings, too, were blown apart.

British North America had felt the shock as well and had seen the onset of the French and Indian War. Earlier, General William Braddock had been defeated by the French and their Indian allies in western Pennsylvania, and troops of both sides would soon be fighting elsewhere in North America. They had just recently clashed in upstate New York and were alert for nightly encroachments by the enemy. We can understand that they were shaky even before the quake. The British garrison at Lake George was aroused by the shock of the Cape Ann quake, as were the French at Ft. St. Frederic at nearby Lake Champlain, who had been recently defeated at Lake George by an army that included many Americans.

Not many soldiers were felled in that battle, but in Boston, many chimneys fell to the earth, and many of those that fell had been built on filled-in land near the waterfront and in the North End, land that had little resistance to earthquakes. Building on this unstable land would have consequences reaching far into the future.

Nearly 100 chimneys fell on filled-in lands, some of them crashing through roofs as well. Roofs, themselves, succumbed, and so did church steeples, some of them leaning in peculiar Pisa-like attitudes, which left Boston looking like a crazy warren of tall buildings rattling from all the tremors.

It became clear to those who would notice, that buildings made of brick or stone were vulnerable in 1755, as they would be today. South of Boston—in Scituate and Pembroke—long crevices opened in the earth, then filled with sand and water. Elsewhere, in Newington, New Hampshire, these crevices were nearly a thousand feet long and several feet wide, while throughout the countryside, stone walls, so popularly associated with New England farms, fell with the first tremors. New England icons were tumbling everywhere.

Even in Boston, the famed Faneuil Hall shivered from the shaking, and its later-to-be-iconic grasshopper weather vane bit the dust. The gilded insect ordinarily rose ten feet above the roof of the then-new (1742) edifice. The shiny, winged insect usually rotated on a pine spindle, but the quake saw to that, snapping the wooden spindle that served as an axis to its airy swimming. The vane clattered down the roof and tumbled to the ground.

Hundreds of roofs were destroyed in Boston, but brick buildings suffered the most damage, some streets being filled with fallen bricks and other debris. But no person or animal was killed. They were, however, terrorized. Cows and horses ran into barns, dogs went to the doors of their owners and howled, flocks of birds rose up suddenly and flew for long periods, refusing to light on the earth or on buildings.

People were scared out of their wits. A writer of the time said:

> I walked out about sunrise, and every face looked ghastly. In fine, some of our solid and pious gentlemen had such an awe and gloom spread over their countenances as would have checked the gay airs of the most intrepid.

Earthquakes are known to be able to destroy one's ordinary confidence because people feel that if the ground under their feet is unstable, then what can they count upon?

The quake was not the first in this part of New England, though it was the first formally recorded. Oral tradition, by way of Rhode Island Indian tribes, spoke of quakes as far back as 1558. The Pequots and Narragansetts had told governor Roger Williams about that quake and about five others that took place during the previous eighty years.

There was not just shaking, there was spin. Over at noble Harvard, John Winthrop IV, great-grandson of the Puritan governor of Massachusetts Bay Colony, and only the second professor in all of North America to hold a chair in science, blamed the quake on a combination of heat and chemical vapors beneath the earth, while many others—more in keeping with the mind set of Winthrop's ancestors—blamed it on God taking vengeance on contemporary sinners. That view would have been popular among the North Shore's many Puritans, who believed in God's wrath and human sin as moving forces, more powerful than those of nature.

For those more intrigued by scientific fact, in can be said that the 1755 Cape Ann quake was computed later to have been a 6.0 to 6.3 on the Richter scale, and the worst ever experienced in New England. Its origins are uncertain, but some scientists speculated that it came as an aftershock to the Great Earthquake of 1755, which, along with a tsunami and fire, had destroyed Lisbon, Portugal eighteen days earlier. Communications being as slow as they were at the time, New Englanders were probably unaware of the earlier devastation.

The Lisbon event struck at 9:40 a.m. on All Saints Day when the many Catholics of Lisbon were attending mass by the thousands on this holy day of obligation. Many were trapped in the rubble, while others who escaped this fate were drowned by the tsunami that swept in from the sea, or perished in the great fire that followed. These circumstances, of course, led to further attributions to the wages of sin, though some pointed out that thousands were in church when they met their demise while fleshpots, like Paris, were spared.

The Lisbon tsunami was not the only one. The Lesser Antilles Islands, off the coast of Venezuela, suffered from one, too, attributed to the Cape Ann quake.

Though much of this was of limited scientific value, it did start people thinking in that direction. After many years, for example, we know today that Boston—and especially its filled-in land, like Back Bay –would still be vulnerable to a large quake, probably to the tune of billions of dollars in damage and the loss of many lives.

We also know, from a recent study of the magnetic field of New England, that the ocean off the coast of Cape Ann has a different pattern of rock formation than the mostly-granite Boston Basin. It has a highly magnetic and circular underwater geology, which is of a dense rock called gabbro, in the form of a cylindrical shape called "plutons" that descend into the earth. These are also found in other areas around the region where earthquakes have happened. And they are found only in those places.

Earthquake Aftershocks

The major earthquake that struck Cape Ann and elsewhere on November 18, 1755, felled chimneys in Boston, smashed stone walls that had stood in the countryside, caused a tsunami to bore into islands hundreds of miles away. It killed no one, but it did shatter lives and created bizarre circumstances both on the North Shore and elsewhere.

Browne's Folly

In Danvers, just northwest of Salem and Peabody, William Browne, a wealthy merchant of Salem, had built a huge estate in the shape of the letter "H," with two wings, each eighty feet long. Browne was clearly no ordinary citizen. He and his wife, Mary Burnet, loved beautiful (and expensive) things.

They also liked showy things, which perhaps indicated a possible flaunting of wealth so that they might be seen in a more positive light.

For example, the couple was the first in town to own a private carriage with handsome livery, which they drove prominently and showily through the streets of Salem for all to see and admire. They also entertained lavishly in a fine mansion built on top of a hill. The estate had a large domed hall where they entertained their guests like a medieval lord and lady. The hall had a wall that was covered by a beautiful tapestry rendered by a Dutch artist. Their noisy revels rang out from their hilltop. But all this wealth, and even the thick walls of masonry that could not keep their sounds of celebration within them, did not render the Brownes or their great estate safe from acts of nature. Its stone edifice was particularly vulnerable to earthquakes…and one would arrive soon and suddenly.

The town of Danvers was, itself, visited by the earthquake, which lasted about five minutes and brought sickening wavelike motions followed by four days of tremors. Chimneys toppled; windowpanes broke. But Browne's fine structure, called "Browne's Folly" by local and perhaps envious folks, was broken into three sections, as if indeed struck by the fist of some supernatural power.

The sad story of the Brownes might have been forgotten in time, but for a famous writer who lived more than 100 years later in the area. He was the famed writer Nathaniel Hawthorne, and he lived on Salem's shores as a boy. Nathaniel remembered the mansion on a hill and memorialized it in a piece he wrote for the benefit of Essex Institute (now part of the Peabody-Essex Museum). In his boyhood, the mansion was known as "Browne's Folly." Quoted from Nathaniel Hawthorne:

> This eminence is a long ridge rising out of the level country around, like a whale's back out of a calm sea, with the head and tail beneath the surface.

Though it had been many years, Hawthorne remembered well the look of the place and its position on the hill above a lane:

> From this lane there is a steep ascent up the side of the hill, the ridge of which affords two views of very wide extent and variety. On one side is the ocean, and Salem and Beverly on its shores; on the other a rural scene, almost perfectly level, so that each man's metes and bounds can be traced out as on a map. The beholder takes in at a glance the estates on which different families have long been situated, and the houses where they have dwelt, and cherished their various interests, intermarrying,

agreeing together, or quarrelling, going to live, annexing little bits of real estate, acting out their petty parts in life, and sleeping quietly under the sod at last. A man's individual affairs look not so very important, when we can climb high enough to get the idea of a complicated neighborhood.

Hawthorne had often gazed at and dreamed about the place, imagining the people who lived there.

But what made the hill particularly interesting to me, were the traces of an old and long-vanished edifice, midway on the curving ridge, and at its highest point. A pre-revolutionary magnate, the representative of a famous old Salem family, had here built himself a pleasure house, on a scale of magnificence, which, combined with its airy site and difficult approach, obtained for it and for the entire hill on which it stood, the traditionary title of "Browne's Folly."

Whether a folly or no, the house was certainly an unfortunate one. While still in its glory, it was so tremendously shaken by the earthquake of 1755 that the owner dared no longer reside in it; and practically acknowledging that its ambitious site rendered it indeed a Folly, he proceeded to locate it on...humbler ground. The great house actually took up its march along the declining ridge of the hill, and came safely to the bottom, where it stood till within the memory of men now alive.

The proprietor, meanwhile, had adhered to the Royalist side, and fled to England during the Revolution. The mansion was left under the care of Richard Derby (an ancestor of the present Derby family), who had a claim to the Browne property through his wife, but seems to have held the premises precisely as the refugee left them, for a long term of years, in the expectation of his eventual return.

The house remained, with all its furniture in its spacious rooms and chambers, ready for the exile's occupancy, as soon as he should reappear. As time went on, however, it began to be neglected, and was accessible to whatever vagrant, or idle school-boy, or berrying party might choose to enter through its ill-secured windows.

Like many large abandoned houses, this one had a ghost story—at least in the minds of the youth of town:

there was one closet in the house, which everybody was afraid to enter, it being supposed that an evil spirit—perhaps a domestic Demon of the Browne family—was confined in it. One day, three or four score years ago, some school-boys happened to be playing in the deserted chambers, and took it into their heads to develop the secrets of this mysterious closet. With great difficulty and tremor they succeeded in forcing the door. As it flew open, there was a vision of people in garments of antique magnificence: gentlemen in curled wigs and tarnished gold-lace, and ladies in brocade and quaint head-dresses, rushing tumultuously forth and tumbling upon the floor. The urchins took to their heels, in huge dismay, but crept back, after a while, and discovered that the apparition was composed of a mighty pile of family portraits. I had the story, the better part of a hundred years afterwards, from the very school-boy who pried open the closet door.

Those same people, who blamed non-Puritan ways for the earthquake, said the Lord had punished Browne for his extravagance. Their beliefs were no doubt reinforced by what followed. Browne vowed never to live on the estate again. The next year, two of Browne's children died of disease. Shortly thereafter, his second wife passed away, and, in 1763 (Hawthorne's version differs here), Browne himself died of apoplexy in a field he owned in Beverly. He had ordered a monument for his tombstone, but it was never put up. The remains of his hilltop estate were removed to the bottom of the hill and then carted away to three different locations. Browne is little remembered; nor is the earthquake.

The Scrubmaid and the Baronet

A young woman from Marblehead, Agnes Surriage, was out of the country when Cape Ann was struck, but an earlier quake affected her life profoundly.

Seventeen days earlier, on November 1, 1755, a disastrous earthquake, perhaps related to the one on the North Shore, struck Lisbon, Portugal. The Cape Ann quake may have brought a tsunami that came to the Leeward Islands, and the Portugal event may have sent vibrations across the ocean. The quake had a profound influence on two prominent people with a North Shore background.

They were an unusual couple to say the least, and they, too, were living in sin, as the Puritans and others of that day would have said. He was the great-great grandson of Oliver Cromwell the great English anti-monarch, and yet his family, back in England, was in favor with the current monarch. His sister had a title and he, himself, had recently become a baronet.

The woman he lived with had a socially mixed background. Her mother had come from a cultured, educated American family descended from John Brown, who had once owned much of Maine, and her father was a Marblehead fisherman. She worked as a sort of scullery maid in an inn that stood on a rocky hill overlooking the harbor in that seaside town.

The inn was named "Fountain Inn" for a deep well that stood nearby. The innkeeper was Nathaniel Barrett, known far and wide for his hospitality and service. Here, on foggy or wintry evenings, fishermen drank their brown ales and told their storm-tossed tales. Here, of a summer afternoon, a handsome coach and four came to a halt, and a footman emerged to open the doors and to help the passenger dismount. He was a richly clad gentleman, the likes of whom had never graced the establishment before.

This was Sir Charles Henry Frankland, His Majesty's Collector of the Port of Boston, and, next to his friend, Governor Shirley, the most prominent personage in the Massachusetts Bay Colony. This refined and well-bred aristocrat had come to Marblehead to oversee the establishment of coastal defenses and would stay at Fountain Inn.

That stay would be auspicious. While there, he descended the stairs one morning when he saw a servant below. She was on her knees scrubbing the floor, a maid of perhaps sixteen. She made way to let him pass and he noticed that her feet were bare. As she bowed and lowered her eyes, Frankland could see that this young woman had a fresh, uncommon beauty.

Oliver Wendell Holmes, who later told their story in verse, wrote:

She turned-a reddening rose in bud,
Its calyx half withdrawn –
Her cheek on fire with damasked blood
Of girlhood's glowing dawn.

He asked her about her parents and learned that she was the middle child of a fisherman of the town. Then he extracted a five-shilling coin from his vest pocket and gave it to her, saying that she should buy some shoes.

A few months later, Franklin was back in Marblehead and at the inn while inspecting the fortifications. On that trip, he went to the home of this young woman, Agnes Surriage, and told her parents that their daughter ought to have greater aspirations, that he wished to arrange for her education and training in the social graces, and that he would pay for this. They agreed, and under the patronage of the governor's wife, Agnes attended school in Boston with the daughters of the wealthy. She learned music, dancing, and domestic skills over a period of four years.

It is clear that at some point the two fell in love. However, Frankland knew that Boston society, and even less, his family in England, would not understand his marrying this woman from well below his station. He made her his "ward" and the two lived together in Boston. Henry or "Harry" was not only socially superior, but ten years Agnes's senior, and the circumstances of their arrangement did not sit well in priggish Boston. He had sculpted his "Pygmalion" into a "Fair Lady." But tongues wagged; he was shunned socially.

While he continued to do business in Boston, Frankland had a grand estate built in Hopkinton, 25 miles west, for him and Agnes. It was the equal and more to that of William Browne in Danvers, boasting 500 acres with a magnificent manor house on a high hill that gave views of Mt. Monadnock in New Hampshire, 100 miles to the north. Like Browne's hilltop estate, Frankland's home had a great hall with tapestried walls.

Here, according to stories, he made a new band of friends, of a distinctly *un-Puritan* persuasion. In that great hall they had great feasts, bacchanalian in nature, with fine wines flowing as though from fountains. It was, perhaps, a pleasant interval for both Henry and Agnes. But it would be short-lived. He had to return to England to contest a lawsuit having to do with the family's holdings there. He took Agnes with him, hoping that her appearance and acculturation would sway his family to acceptance of her.

He would be disappointed. Agnes might just as well have had Hawthorne's "Scarlet Letter" branded upon her, so distasteful was she to these haughty aristocrats. Henry decided to leave England. He and Agnes went to Lisbon, where they lived among a colony of English ex-patriots who had gone abroad for various reasons. Many were non-religious and followed lifestyles similar to those of Frankland's friends in Hopkinton. Significantly, the English colony was on high ground, safer from natural disasters.

November 1, 1755 was All Saints Day in a city with six cathedrals and many other Catholic churches. The day was a holy day with many of the trappings of a holiday. The streets were filled with people, and Henry wanted to join them. He set out in a carriage, accompanied by a wealthy English noblewoman. Agnes remained at home.

At 10 a.m., on a perfectly clear day, the rumbling, catastrophic earthquake, measuring a 9 or higher on the Richter Scale began, lasting from 4.5 to 6 minutes. In the ancient city, 85 per cent of the buildings were destroyed; 60,000 people died. People ran out of buildings and headed for the waterfront where no buildings could fall on them. But shortly, a giant tsunami roared up the Tagus River and drowned many of them, even driving sizable ships onto the shore. It was followed by a devastating fire that raged for five days.

As Frankland, in his carriage, passed through the streets, the palace of a Portuguese nobleman fell from its foundation into the street, burying the carriage and its passengers under rubble. Frankland later recalled that his immediate sensation was of the noblewoman grabbing him and sinking her teeth through his coat. Though they called out, cries like theirs were everywhere and panicky people were trying to save themselves. Trapped in this hopeless situation, unable to move, Frankland had ample time to examine his life and the life he had given to Agnes. This All Saints Day was a perfect time for examination of conscience.

Agnes, meanwhile, was on safer ground. When the earthquake came, she had the presence to stuff her pockets with all the gold she could find and headed out to look for Henry. She knew the route he had planned to take, but had to find her way through streets, now filled with rubble, and to thread her way through crowds of erratic citizens. After two hours, she began to climb over one huge hill of debris and heard Henry's muted cries. She tried to dig him out with her bare hands.

Despite her years as a housemaid, she lacked the strength for this task. She took out the gold she had carried and managed to convince a group of sailors from one of the ships that had been tossed ashore to help her, and eventually, she freed Henry and his companion from their certain graves.

Liberated, in more than one way, Henry, who had done all that thinking and perhaps praying, sought and found a Catholic priest, and he and Agnes were married, even as the disaster continued. A few weeks later, they returned to England and were married again by an Anglican clergyman on board the ship, thus making the marriage valid in the eyes of his relatives. This time, Henry's mother and sister embraced the woman who had saved his life.

The couple returned to Boston in 1756, where Lady Frankland was now received readily by the polite society that had earlier rejected her. Her cultured personality was now appreciated. They purchased a mansion on Garden Court Street, in Boston's North End, where they lived for a year. Known as the finest house in the city, it was later called the Clark-Frankland House. They hired a French cook and entertained lavishly there. The baronet often entertained himself by riding his pony up and down the home's wide staircases.

Having finally overcome the bad memories associated with his encounter with the earthquake, Henry and Agnes returned to Lisbon for several years, where he served as Consul General.

In 1763, they returned to Hopkinton. Next, they moved to Bath, in England, where Henry died in 1768. Lady Frankland then returned to

The couple later lived in this fine house in Boston's North End.

Hopkinton until the American Revolution began. Then, as a loyalist, she decided to return to England.

These Loyalists or "Tories" had some influence on the British, who controlled the besieged Boston. General Gage often gave in to the Tory element in Boston when they presented him with their demands. Though he allowed passage in and out of the town, he would allow no more than thirty wagons to enter at one time.

Lady Frankland was a notable exception. Appearing in the Roxbury lines, and ready to cross Boston Neck with her entourage, she was stopped by the lieutenant in charge, but was allowed to enter with her seven trunks after producing a permit signed by Benjamin Church. The lieutenant was later reprimanded. In addition, she was allowed to have all her beds and furniture brought in, all her boxes and crates, plus a basket of chickens and a bag of corn, two barrels and a hamper, two horses and chaises, along with all the articles in the chaise, excepting arms and ammunition, one phaeton, some tongues (ham and veal), and sundry small bundles. Her pigs and several of her livestock were not permitted to enter, but, on the whole, this incident offers us a look at how money and position reigned, even in a town under siege. Once before, in Lisbon, Agnes had used gold to help her in a crisis. It was a lesson well-learned.

Back in England, as Agnes Frankland, the former Marblehead floor-scrubber was now warmly welcomed by Harry's relatives. In due course, she married a country banker and died in England in 1783.

⚓

Cape Ann
Before the Earthquake

The Puritans who saw the earthquake as an act of God (see page 10) and the splendid display of the Brownes (see page 11) as offensive to Him, had been the major part of the population on Cape Ann, and indeed, around Boston, since early in the previous century. But they had not been the first people to live there, or even the first Europeans to explore its reaches.

That honor went to a French explorer. Samuel de Champlain became the first European to set foot on Cape Ann when he explored the Atlantic coast, from Newfoundland south to Cape Cod, and later became known as "The Father of New France," for his exploration and settlement in Quebec. Champlain came ashore at Gloucester where he met the resident Native Americans. He also drew a map of the harbor which he called "le beau port," but that name didn't stick.

The first Englishman to sail this shore was John Smith, a name well-remembered, but a person little-known. His wild adventures in Jamestown, Virginia, have been bruited about, and he deserves credit for his part in saving that colony. But that was not an end to his achievement.

In addition to his adventures in Jamestown, Virginia, Smith earned fame in another way. He excelled at drawing maps, where there had been no maps, and at writing books and pamphlets that publicized his findings. His work led both Pilgrims and Puritans to America. It was the Puritans who came to Cape Ann and who were the mainstays of the Massachusetts Bay Colony.

THE PORTRAICTUER OF CAPTAYNE IOHN SMITH
ADMIRALL OF NEW ENGLAND

These are the Lines that shew thy Face but those
That shew thy Grace and Glory, brighter bee
Thy Faire-Discoueries and Fowle-Overthrowes
Of Salvages, much Civilliz'd by thee
Best shew thy Spirit and to it Glory Wyn;
So thou art Brasse without but Golde within.

Adventurer and explorer, John Smith's exploits received less attention than the myths that are told about him.

In 1614, Smith, an adventurer and explorer had mapped the peninsula north of Boston and, in fact, all of Massachusetts Bay and north to Maine. He wanted to learn and promulgate the possibilities for fishing, trading, and settlement. Smith realized that this was the right time for the English to colonize New England, and he said so in his *Description of New England,* which was widely read. It described the fish, soils, plant and animal life, climate, and people of the region.

A decade later, thirty-two members of the Dorchester Company came from England and set up a fishing post on Cape Ann, in 1624. They (and Smith) had chosen well. The waters were near the Stellwagen Bank, one of the best fishing areas in the world. It stretches from Cape Ann to Cape Cod and is today a National Marine Sanctuary.

The first settlement did not last, but the Dorchester Company became part of the Massachusetts Bay Colony. They understood it was controlled by the Puritans, but King Charles I, who granted a charter in 1629, seemed to think it was just another stock company, as so many colonies had been. The Puritans of that day were fleeing England for religious freedom and meant to establish a religious colony where they settled. They came, 20,000 strong, in the next few years as part of what was called "The Great Migration." They came with John Winthrop, who had been chosen as governor, and their first landfall was Salem.

The Puritans quickly decided that Salem was not the right place, so they kept looking. Winthrop and a large party moved from there to Charlestown in 1630. Within the decade, Puritan villages had been settled up and down the North Shore, as well as farther south.

These settlements followed a pattern. Wherever they sprang up, the people had their meetinghouse at the center of the community. The farms were on the outskirts, and the usual pattern was to have a village green with a church at one end and houses built around it. That's why so many New England towns still have those features.

Winthrop and his followers came on a mission. They believed that the Puritans were God's chosen people, and that they must set an example for all who came to America. In order to follow God's will, they believed, one must read the Bible, and it followed that their children must learn to read so that they, too, could read the Bible. So education was important in New England and schools were set up, including a college in Cambridge that was, in time, named Harvard College for John Harvard who had willed his library to the school.

Strong religious beliefs were one thing, but these early settlers had to eke out a living on the "…stern and rock-bound coast…" of New England. The way they did it is a hallmark of the early settlers of this area. Farming and fishing were seasonal things on the rocky coast of Massachusetts, and settlers learned to use their own skills. The term associated with their attitude is "Yankee Ingenuity," a way to make the things they needed. During the American Revolution and the War of 1812, when manufactured goods from abroad were hard to get, people living here began manufacturing on a large scale, using waterpower provided by rivers in the area.

The seaport towns also admitted many immigrants, mostly from Europe. Many of the towns in the area found room for them, including the towns and cities along the coast north of Boston as far as Cape Ann. We'll offer a historic sketch of each, mention some of the prominent people and events, and pay attention to the trends we have mentioned.

Those trends were some of the major influences for in American History prior to the 20th century, but notable "firsts" took place in this area in the later period as well. As you read through the following pages, you'll be taking another look at our nation's growth and the way it began here and flowered everywhere.

To the author, the "story" part of "history" is important. There will also be plenty of stories that make up the lore of the region—stories that will stick with you and which you can then pass along.

⚓

Salisbury

FUN IN THE SUN

The town of Salisbury, home to the Pentucket native tribe, was first settled by English colonists in 1638. Since it is at the mouth of the Colchester River, its first name was Merrimack, but that was quickly renamed Salisbury, after the historic town in southern England near Stonehenge.

The first settlers were fairly isolated and few in number, so they had to trust one another for their defense. They feared the Indians, and therefore made their roads into a semicircle that would let them reach their fort or garrison house quickly in the event of an attack.

But, as in other coastal towns, the numbers of the tribe had been decimated by European diseases. The colonists' greater danger came from packs of wolves whose object was killing and carrying off their livestock. The cattle and sheep were essential to the settlers, too, so the wolves had to be driven off. The pattern of the roads may still be seen in a triangular shape near the town center, but the wolves were last seen slinking away into the past.

The town planning was typical of many 17th century coastal towns. Each colonist was apportioned land for a house lot near the town center, as well as a lot just outside the center for farming and grazing. Their animals subsisted largely on the hay from salt marshes, of which Salisbury had an abundance. Consequently, residents also got a "sweepage lot" which was a large section near the beach for harvesting hay.

Boats were later built along the river, and the town prospered due to its position between Portsmouth and Newburyport, a line followed later when railroads were built. The access later allowed people with leisure time to vast the beaches and spend vacation time along the shore.

Salisbury owns a part of the Great Marsh, with mudflats where clams are taken, but is perhaps known best for its 20th-century role as a summer resort with a thriving amusement park that included a carousel (called The Flying Horse, hand carved and established in 1914), a Dodgem ride, and The Sky Rocket, Salisbury Beach's first roller coaster. Most of these operated from 1914 to 1980, when the beach also hosted concerts with current favorites like Glenn Miller, Frank Sinatra, Ella Fitzgerald, and Louis Armstrong. The last amusement, Pirate's Fun Park, closed in 2004. It was replaced by condominiums. Almost ninety percent of the town's geographic area is open space, including Salisbury Beach State Reservation.

The Dodgem, installed in 1920, turned out to be more than expected by its inventor, Max Stoehrer. Motor cars were new, but starting to surge in that day, though many people had not yet driven one. They had caught the fancy of Americans, and Stoehrer decided to build a small, two-person car, run on electricity in an amusement park, to provide the feeling of actually driving a car.

Once the location of a fine amusement park, including this one, Salisbury, near the New Hampshire border, still boasts a fine, popular beach. *Postcard by Thomson & Thomson, 1914.*

As he thought about his invention, he realized that his car would be hard to steer, especially by inexperienced drivers. That meant that cars penned up in a fenced area would have trouble avoiding one another, so he called his invention "the Dodgem." When he turned them loose, customers decided it was more fun running into each other and the big, padded bumpers would make them relatively safe. Today, they might be a trial lawyer's delight, but Stoehrer's installation, at the corner of Driftway and Ocean Front Streets, was a big success and lasted until 1975.

Salisbury also had a category of amusement called "dark rides." These came in many forms and often had dark tunnels with scary surprises lurking within them. Some had seafaring themes, especially pirates. One was Pirate's Fun Park, which lasted until 1999, and another was Kastle Frankenstein. (Revere Beach had Bluebeard's Castle, also a pirate theme.)

While the amusements are gone, the beach remains and so does its popularity, maintaining Salisbury's leisure-time traditions.

⚓

Newburyport

RIDING THE WAVES OF HISTORY

Newburyport, at the mouth of the Merrimack River, thirty-five miles north of Boston, has a varied history and a story that is still being told. Its earliest history is that of the Pawtucket Indians of the region and then of the farming community known as Newbury.

Beginning along the Parker River, Newbury expanded toward the ocean, setting out a new town along the Merrimack where residents (mostly merchants) exchanged their farms for new lands close to the ocean.

In that location, the residents naturally turned to the sea to make a living, building ships, fishing, and trading, with over a hundred ships being built before the 18th century was yet two decades old. The ships were used in coastal trade and for trade with Europe and the islands of the Caribbean.

Newburyport became a haven for the "Triangle Trade," bringing molasses from the West Indies in exchange for lumber and fish and other goods, and distilling it locally into rum. The rum was traded for slaves who were brought from the West Indies. Slavery, however, was not popular in Newburyport, where abolitionism had many contributors to the Underground Railroad aiding escaped slaves. The abolitionist leader, William Lloyd Garrison, was born here and a statue of him stands in Brown Square, where abolitionist meetings were often held.

In 1764, Newburyport separated from Newbury in a dispute over the location of a meetinghouse—a common reason for such separations in those days. While trade and other seafaring activities dominated Newburyport through the 19th century, the town also attracted tradesmen, artisans, and merchants.

Hard times came to Newburyport during the War for Independence. The ships could no longer trade with the British, but shipowners took to privateering—capturing British ships for the value of their cargoes. This was no easy task for lightly-armed vessels built for trade and not warfare. Twenty-four ships and a thousand men were lost at this time.

However, when the war ended, prosperity came calling once more. The decades up through the Federal Period (until approximately 1810) were the heyday for early Newburyport. Its sailing fleet, once depleted, grew by a third and its population doubled. New homes were built, too, mostly along High Street.

But the ups and downs of the town's fortunes took a lower pitch again just after this peak of prosperity. British interference with American ships and sailors led to President Thomas Jefferson's Embargo Act in 1807, and then to the War of 1812. Trade was ruined and the docks stood quietly idle. Then in 1811, fire destroyed most of the business district, though it was quickly rebuilt with buildings in the latest style.

The stymied ocean trade remained a drag on the town's commerce until the 1830s, when textile mills were built, transforming the economy to a manufacturing center. However, shipbuilding would have a renaissance. Since the port was at the mouth of the Merrimack and many mills were located upstream, raw materials could be downloaded on the docks of Newburyport, using local shipping. Those ships could and did also become part of the Gold Rush, when young men from the East sought quick transportation to the gold fields of California. That period of shipbuilding lasted until the opening years of the 20th century. The last ship was built in 1901 in Newburyport, closing a 250-year period of history. But more lie ahead.

The railroad was next, arriving in 1840, and establishing termini for the storage and distribution of coal. The town became a city in 1851, and its borders were broadened to reach from Plum Island to the Artichoke River.

Mary L. Cushing, launched 1863, Newburyport.
Library of Congress, published between 1900 and 1920.

This barrier island runs from the Merrimack River to the Ipswich River. The resort area is subject to severe erosion. *Postcard 1906.*

In addition to textiles, the city had a significant shoemaking industry, but decline lay ahead yet again, when the mills closed.

The economic tides ran in and out at Newburyport, but the city found a way to ride a cresting wave time and again. By the middle of the 20th century, when it was in the doldrums, the city at the mouth of the Merrimack began a rebirth, but it took a different turn from other cities of that day that went whole hog along the ruinous path of urban renewal. Rather than tear down homes and raze buildings, Newburyport renewed those structures that dated to the fire of 1811 and restored the city, with help from federal funds. The result of this was a proud architectural heritage of New England's Federal times.

Today's State Street and the surrounding area exhibit some of the finest examples of architecture of the early 19th century, a model example of historic preservation.

⚓

Rowley

MILLS AND MOLLUSKS

When it was settled by Rev. Ezekiel Rogers and twenty families, in 1639, Rowley was larger than it is today, since it included parts of Haverhill, Boxford, Groveland, Byfield, Middleton, and Georgetown. In addition to the passengers, the sailing ship *John of London*, also brought the first printing press in America, equipment that was later used at Harvard College. The town was named for Rogers' hometown in Yorkshire, where he had been let go as pastor for being a Puritan. He then became pastor of Rowley, Massachusetts.

Four years later, the men of Rowley built the first fulling mill in the colonies on the Mill River, as well as a stone bridge with an arch and keystone made of granite and using no mortar. They also built a dam. Rowley became famous for its fine hemp, flax, and cotton. A sawmill, built in 1669, still operates. In the 19th century, a wagon factory was added, and by the end of that century, the town made many shoes and also had a boat- and dory-building business.

Nonetheless, many of the early settlers were farmers and fishermen who built simple homes around the common, an area also used as a training field for the militia. From there, the expedition to attack Quebec during the Revolution was led by Benedict Arnold. That area and other streets in the town still have many old homes from the colonial period.

As in other coastal areas, the salt marshes were an important component of town life for early and later settlers. The hay found there was shared by landowners and used to feed livestock, as well as for insulation for houses, roofing, and to cover the floors of stables, since it did not burn as quickly as other hay. The dairy cattle who ate the hay gave richer milk. The hay is used today mostly for mulch. The coastal flatlands produce some of the best shellfish, especially clams, in the world.

⚓

Ipswich

CLAMS, CRANE, AND A CASTLE

It's not surprising that the town best known for its clams is on the coast of Massachusetts. That town is Ipswich, whose history goes back to John Smith's description of it and the settling by the Winthrops in 1633. Smith, a prolific writer, said nothing about clams, but he did mention the sands, writing:

> there are many sands at the entrance of the Harbour... Here are many rising hills, and on their tops and descents are many corn fields and delightful groves... plain marsh ground, fit for pasture, or salt ponds. There is also Oakes, Pines, Walnuts, and other wood to make this place an excellent habitation, being a good and safe harbour.

Residing on those hills and lands were Indians, who called the area "Agawam." The tribes had lived there for millennia—carbon dating indicates they had been there for more than nine centuries. However, their tenure was coming to an end. Disease had reduced their ranks, and they presented little threat to the colonists, who first settled in 1633 under the leadership of John Winthrop, son of the Puritan governor, who had arrived on the ship *Arabella*. Among that small group were prominent men, such as Richard Dudley, lieutenant governor, and Richard Saltonstall, whose family would be influential through the 20th century. They called the settlement "Ipswich" after a town in Suffolk, England.

This place gained another name in 1687—"The Birthplace of American Liberty." The townspeople protested a tax imposed by the Royal Governor, John Andros, arguing that, as Englishmen, "taxation without representation" was unacceptable. Andros had some of them thrown in jail, but two years later he was recalled to England and the town got a new charter.

Ipswich had developed a small cottage industry of lace making, but in 1822, a stocking-making machine was brought from England, in contravention of regulations which forbade bringing machines out of England. Textile mills did not spring up at once, but little by little over the years until, in 1868,

Ipswich, north of Cape Ann, features the oldest double-arched bridge in North America. *Courtesy Library of Congress, published between 1900 and 1920.*

Amos Lawrence established the Ipswich Hosiery Mills in a stone mill on the Ipswich River, using its water power for what became, by 1900, the largest stocking mill in the country.

However, the town did not grow much from that time forward, although it did have many European immigrants, as did other New England towns, and much of its housing stock remains from earlier times. In fact, Ipswich has more houses from the pre-1725 years than any town in the country.

The town's long shoreline contains many tidal estuaries and salt marshes, and it has well-known reserves at the Parker Wildlife Sanctuary and Crane's Beach.

And, of course, there are those famous clams, part of the extensive shellfish commerce of the town.

A Chicago plumber with a taste for the ornamental and grand, brought a notable site to the town. In 1910, Richard Crane bought Castle Hill, a drumlin that overlooks Ipswich Bay, and hired the Olmsted Brothers, successors to famed landscape architect Frederick Law Olmsted, to landscape his 3,500-acre estate. He brought in the famed architectural firm of Shepley, Rutan & Coolidge from Boston to design a villa on the hilltop. It would be Italian Renaissance Revival that looked down upon a *grande allee*, a grassy promenade 160 feet wide, bordered with statuary and running a half mile to the sea with wonderful vistas.

The grounds and the vista were fine for Florence, wife of Richard Crane, but she could not abide the house itself, so Thomas promised to replace it in ten years if she still didn't like it. She didn't; so he did—replace it—with a mansion of fifty-nine rooms, built in 1929 (when others were losing their fortunes) and designed by David Adler of Chicago in the English Stuart style. It was called simply "The Great House." The property is now owned by the Trustees of Reservations, who also own Crane Beach. They use the house for concerts and weddings. Additionally, there is an inn on the property and tours are held.

While Castle Hill is the most spectacular of the holdings, and Crane Beach is perhaps the best known, the Crane Wildlife Refuge is a sprawling area that includes seven islands, all of these in the estuary of the Essex River. They are surrounded by the Great Marsh, which is the largest salt marsh in New England, running from Gloucester north to beyond the New Hampshire border, an area of 25,000 acres.

The center of town has many old and historic buildings. *Postcard 1906.*

⚓

Essex

SHELLFISH AND SUMMER PURSUITS

Perhaps the best-known and most coveted seafood from the North Shore are Ipswich clams, though they may not always come from Ipswich. In fact, the fried clam's origin is usually attributed to nearby Essex. Not only that, but Ipswich clams are generally considered any that come from the Great Marsh, off the shores of Ipswich, Essex, Rowley, Newbury, and Newburyport, and feed on the same plankton. They then may be reasonably considered Ipswich clams. Moreover, the beds are periodically closed and clams can be in short supply, so clams from Maine and Cape Cod are often substituted.

The claim for the invention of the fried clam goes back to "Chubby" Woodman, who built a restaurant on Main Street in Essex in 1914. He sold groceries and fresh clams, but the big draw was his deep-fried potato chips which customers were munching and crunching by the bagful. However, on July 3rd, 1916, the chip was replaced by another deep-fried product, largely as the result of a tossed-off joke that generated few laughs. As the lore goes, the store was nearly empty when a regular customer, a fisherman named Tarr, walked in and asked about business. Woodman told him it was "…slower than a couple of snails headed uphill."

Tarr rejoined, "Why don't you fry up some of your clams? If they're as tasty as those potato chips of yours, you'll never have to worry about having enough customers."

Other customers in the store ridiculed Tarr, one reminding him that clams come in shells. Tarr replied, "I wasn't serious, it was just a little joke. I know you can't fry clams like chips!" (In fact, "fried clams" were on the menu of Boston's Parker House as early as 1865, though we don't know if they were deep-fried. Perhaps this news had not reached Essex.

Joke or not, Woodman had vats of fat on the premises for frying his chips, so he and his wife decided there was no harm in trying. They used various batters and liked the way they smelled, so they tried them out on some customers who proclaimed that the clams were delicious. The next day was the July 4th parade, and Woodman had a new product to sell which became the hit of the event. In fact, they became so popular that Howard Johnson, who owned 100 restaurants, came to Essex to see for himself how to make them.

Ipswich clams are whole clams, belly and all, deep-fried in a crumb crust, typically salted, and invariably delicious. They are a staple in New England restaurants, especially on the North Shore where they are often accompanied by lobster rolls.

The shellfish industry provides the largest part of the town's income, along with restaurants, recreational pursuits, and other aspects of tourism. Another source of income here is the sale of antiques. Essex has more antique shops per square mile than any town in the country.

Essex became a town in 1819. Previously, it had been part of Ipswich and was called Chebacco Parish. The parish had lobbied for independent status and the right to build a meetinghouse, which would have made it autonomous. Permission was denied and a law was made which stated that "… no man shall raise a meeting house." But a local woman, Madam Varney, got the women of the town together and they built the meetinghouse while the men watched.

The town of Essex had a thriving shipbuilding trade up into the early part of the 20th century, making many of the schooners used in Gloucester and other towns. The Essex Shipbuilding Museum recalls that tradition. Even today, a shipyard that has been run by the Story Family still builds wooden ships in the established style.

⚓

Rockport

A CHUNK OF GRANITE AND AN ARTISTS' COLONY

As John Smith explored the coast along Cape Ann, he anchored in Sandy Bay, off Rockport, where he raised his bearded chin, lifted his spyglass, and spotted the homes of Indians on the horizon beyond a headland and three islands. He recorded his observations of the area that is now Rockport. That was just prior to the time when widespread epidemics killed most of the American Indians of the coastal area.

For many years, Rockport was just a part of Gloucester—a part where hardly anyone lived. Nonetheless, it was an area that had useful resources. Timber was the main one. Even when few people lived in Rockport, thick stands of pine were being cut for shipbuilding.

At the same time, another resource provided sustenance for those who lived in the new seacoast communities of the Bay State's Atlantic coast. That, of course, was fish. Just off the coast, abundant schools of fish could be found, and, before long, a dock would be built in Sandy Bay from which early settlers could fish and load timber. By the end of the 1700s, the stone for which Rockport was named was being taken, and, by the 1830s, granite was being shipped to other places.

By then, Rockport had a few large estates that were used as summer places, and it had a fishing village. The southern part of Cape Ann, however, primarily Gloucester, were becoming quite populated. In 1840, it had become clear that Rockport and Gloucester were turning into two quite different places.

During the Industrial Revolution, the demand for Rockport's granite became even greater. Transporting it great distances became the challenge. Since it was on the coast, shipping via sea made sense, and a special kind of sloop was invented, a sailing vessel that was built to haul large slabs of stone.

As it did in Quincy and other quarrying communities, the growing granite industry drew immigrants from Sweden and Finland. These men came from a tradition of stone working and were skilled in this work, which they also enjoyed. In many cases, generations of the same family had carried on this

Essex Town Hall (Library of Congress)
Essex, and the North Shore are famed for their fried clams, begun here at Woodman's, and still famous today. *Courtesy Library of Congress, Prints & Photographs Division, MA-1222-4*

work and they were lured to Rockport by quarry owners who were able to offer them productive work that they were good at, as well as good pay.

The problem with extractive industries like mining and quarrying is that the raw material eventually runs out, and that happened here, too. Over time, the granite became harder to extract, then demand fell off, and the industry declined. Without an industry based on its natural resources, Rockporters had to find another way to prosper.

It still had its good location, and that would provide an answer. With its craggy rocks, its harbor, seashore and beaches, and an unobstructed view of the eastern sunrises and sunsets, Rockport appealed to potential artists who wanted to capture these things with their oils and watercolors. Beyond the natural views were the things associated with the sea, and these began to fill canvases as well—things like boats and buoys and fishing shacks, including an improbable masterpiece of a red shack on Bradley Wharf that was painted so often it became known as "Motif Number 1," since it was the favorite subject for many of these artists.

Perhaps, incidentally, Rockport became a "dry" town in the 1850s, one of only fifteen in the whole country. It stayed dry until recently, when the town relented somewhat and allowed the serving of alcohol in restaurants, though it still has no liquor stores.

⚓

Gloucester

THEY WHO GO DOWN TO THE SEA IN SHIPS

As we have seen, French explorer Champlain was the first European to land on Cape Ann during his exploration of the coast from Newfoundland to Cape Cod. It was at Gloucester where he met the Native Americans who lived in those parts. His name for it, "le beau port" had no staying power. Nor did the name given to the peninsula by John Smith just a bit later. If "le beau port" was French and unfamiliar, then Smith's "Tragabigzranda" was Greek and even more so.

Smith, a romantic adventurer who lived enough thrilling episodes to spark a long-running television action series, came up with that troublesome name during a period when he was being held in prison by the Turks. A Greek maiden by that name had helped him to escape, so a cape was named for her—at least for a short time. Not impartial to Greek names, Smith also named three offshore islands for the three Turks who he had beheaded during his escape. Smith's maps were filled with references to his world-wide exploits, but few of them would endure.

John Smith used a lot of Indian names, too, but when he presented his maps to Prince Charles of England, who would later be King Charles I, Smith told the Prince to change any names he didn't like. The Prince went at it with his (presumably) blue pencil and replaced them with names that were more to his liking. However, only four of these remain, including the place he named for his mother, Queen Anne of Denmark. On the map, it became "Cape Ann."

By 1617, the Native Americans, who Champlain had met and who had filled the lens of Smith's spyglass, had lost three out of every four of their numbers to disease. The countrymen of those Europeans who had brought the diseases continued to arrive. At first it was those abundant codfish that brought them. The English from the Dorchester Company caught cod and then landed on Cape Ann to dry their catch. They did not settle permanently, but as we have seen, the Puritans who came during the Great Migration did. They knew how to fish, too, and they also tried farming. Some of these got titles to their lands from the governor of Massachusetts Bay—enough so that Gloucester was established as a town in 1642.

The Schooner and her Skippers

With all this seafaring, it was only natural that shipbuilding would follow, and early in the 1700s, it did. Builders at Gloucester and Essex made masts from the tall oak trees that stood in plentiful numbers, as though grown for just this purpose. These shipbuilders, in fact, became so good at their craft that they specialized, inventing a new type of sailing vessel designed for the work that they did.

Homer's oil-on-canvas captured all manner of boat from sail to dory in this busy harbor scene, 1873.

Drying fish in Gloucester Harbor. This scene was common to many North Shore sites, but nowhere more fitting than Gloucester, home of the fisherman. *Postcard 1915.*

Invented in 1713, the new style ship was called a "schooner." Schooners had fore and aft sails on two masts or more, with the forward one being the taller. Andrew Robinson built the first one. According to legend, an observer exclaimed, "Oh, how she scoons!" using a word derived from a Scots word that means skipping along the surface of the water. They may not really have *scooned*, but they seemed to. Schooners moved fast, and could get to the fishing grounds and back quickly, hauling their catch. That meant they were worth their weight in gold, or fish, anyway.

The schooners gave North Shore fishermen an advantage over their competitors. The schooner was also used for foreign trade, and all this fishing and trading made Gloucester dependent on the sea. Gloucester developed a marine culture. It not only had scores of schooners tied up at its docks, but it looked and smelled like a fishing town. It soon had many shops and naval-based businesses, like rope making, chandleries, and, of course, salted fish—it's main product. Their trading was mostly with ports in the West Indies, from which they took wine, molasses, and sugar. The molasses was used to make rum, while plantation owners used the salt fish to feed their slaves. So, like most New England ports, the trading of slaves was abetted on Cape Ann.

In 1849, John Pew and Sons, a seafood firm, was established. It exists today as the famed Gorton's of Gloucester. Also in the 19th century, fishermen from the Azores and Italy came to Gloucester and their descendants stayed for generations, lending their traditions to such things as fishing and religious festivals.

Gloucester's men also fought in the American Revolution, often using their fast schooners as privateers to intercept British supply ships bound for Boston. They lost many men, and the fishing fleet was decimated. Fishing by itself was dangerous, without having enemy ships trying to destroy you. In its years, over 10,000 Gloucester men have been lost at sea. Their names have been placed on a large mural in the stairwell of City Hall and on a new memorial as well. The statue of the Gloucester fisherman at the helm is an attraction in Gloucester harbor.

Still, the fishing industry thrived and ship-owners and captains built houses overlooking the harbor and all its activity. One part of the fishing industr today is frozen fish. Clarence Birdseye established his frozen fish (later frozen foods) factory at the harbor. He was a visionary, and he did what other visionaries have done. He noticed something in one situation and found a way to transfer it to another. In his case, he had worked in Labrador where he saw members of the

Inuit tribe fishing through holes in the ice. When they pulled out the fish, they instantly froze in the sub-zero temperatures.

He realized that quick freezing was the way to preserve freshness, where slow freezing had failed because that method produced larger ice crystals and a loss of flavor. The Birdseye plant at Gloucester Harbor is closed, and has been sold, but its future is undecided.

Gloucester also thrived as an art colony, thanks to the railroad from Boston, its seascapes and natural beauty making it a favorite of artists, such as Winslow Homer.

In the middle of the 18th century, the granite industry began as it did in Rockport, using immigrants from Finland, Sweden, and Ireland, as well as stone sloops to transport the stone to east coast locations.

Castle of the Father of Remote Control

Gloucester has one point of interest that's quite unusual for a fishing port or even an art colony. Hammond Castle was built by a famous and wealthy inventor known as "The Father of Remote Control." John Hays Hammond, Jr. had the means and the opportunity to channel his life in whatever directions he chose, and his wide-flung and interesting experiences influenced those choices profoundly. In this regard, it was a life most anyone would have chosen, given the chance.

Although he was born in San Francisco, John and his family moved to South Africa, where his father was a mining engineer. Then, while he was still a boy, they moved to England where John became interested in castles and medieval history.

After their return to America, the family visited Thomas Edison in his New Jersey laboratory. Edison took an interest in young John because he asked so many questions. Edison took him on a tour of his laboratory and he became John's mentor, as did Alexander Graham Bell later in John's life.

When grown, Hammond went to Yale University and studied at the Sheffield Scientific School, where he learned about radio waves, met A. G. Bell, and became his protégé until the time of Bell's death. When he graduated, Hammond took a job at the U.S. Patent Office. He had learned from Edison that it was important to make money from your inventions and to protect them with a patent. Edison had always been keen on patenting his work, and Bell defended his patent for the telephone over 600 times. Hammond, too, became an expert in the patenting process.

John Hammond then started his own laboratory for radio research on his father's estate in Gloucester. Hammond would be credited with over 400 inventions, the most for any American other than Edison. He served on the board of Radio Corporation of America (RCA), met most of the best-known scientists and socialites, and added to his already considerable fortune.

He also fulfilled his interest in castles and things historic. Between 1925 and 1929, he built his castle (with a working drawbridge) in Gloucester. He lived in the castle and ran his laboratory there as well. In his "castle by the sea," he invented the remote control, giving, in time, a new meaning to the seaside term "surfing." Hammond Castle became a showplace for his art collection, with its pieces of Medieval, Renaissance, and Roman artifacts—even ancient tombstones and a large pipe organ. The castle sits today on the coast of the Atlantic and serves as a museum. Tradition says it is haunted, and it does have big activities on Halloween.

Hammond Castle is located in the Magnolia section of town, an area south of the town proper and adjacent to Manchester-by-the-Sea. It borders on the ocean and seems like a separate town. Magnolia has many large estates and historical buildings, as well as its own beach.

⚓

Manchester-by-the-Sea
THE BEACH SINGS, BUT THE TOWN IS QUIET

The North Shore town of Manchester-by-the-Sea was first settled in 1629 with passengers from the ship *Talbot*, one of six ships that left England bound for Massachusetts Bay Colony. As with other seacoast places in Massachusetts,

Native Americans arrived there first. These were the Agawams, a branch of the Algonquin tribe, but they too were wiped out by diseases they contracted from European fishermen.

The first group of settlers took care of their immediate needs, establishing a tide mill in 1644, the year before the town was incorporated, and later a grist mill and a saw mill. The town became "Manchester" in 1645, at the request of the people of "Jeoffereyes Creeke." Up to that date, it had been part of Salem. Payments were made to the Indians for the land, and by 1700, the final debt was paid, the Native Americans relinquishing all claims at that point.

The new community set up some laws that were extraordinary for a place of that era. For example, the slave trade was prohibited, as were cruelty to animals and imprisonment of debtors. These morally-based laws were accompanied by others, that seem more like ill-conceived attempts by later legislatures to regulate behavior. For example, there were laws against wearing too much clothing, or the "immodest laying out of…haire," and one about conducting a courtship. The slavery and cruelty issues seemed like a good start, but once these people got going on law-making, they didn't seem able to stop. It was as though they set out to prohibit things that people ought not to do, and having succeeded to their own delight, went on to legislate behavior that they, the legislators, preferred. One could note that history changes, but human nature does not.

The mills were a good start, too. However, an early sign of the area's future was John Norton's use of some of the land that had been granted to him. In 1684, he set up a shipyard, and that became a means for the town to prosper. For the most part, town residents farmed or fished—but mostly they fished. They took a lot of cod, and some mackerel, too, and they became good seamen. By the year 1810, fifty of them owned their own vessels. These were mainly fishing boats, and the town also had fish yards and a storage warehouse for fish. At one point, more than forty sea captains lived in the town.

When the fishing industry died out, the town found other ways to continue. In 1845, and continuing until today, Manchester residents provided summer homes for the wealthy. It began when Boston writer Richard Henry Dana, Jr. (author of *Two Years Before the Mast*—which seems a suitable title for a fishing town) built a fine vacation home there, and other second homes followed. Some of the people taking advantage of this were in government, and many were from the theatre.

Even today, many have summer homes in Manchester and it has also become a year-round residential community. It became "Manchester-by-the-Sea" to distinguish it from the other "Manchesters" in New England. The use of the term seemed a little snobby to Dr. Oliver Wendell Holmes, and when he wrote to his friends who were summering in the North Shore town, he addressed his letters as coming from "Boston-by-the-Charles."

The summer residents enjoyed an unusual beach, called "Singing Beach" for its sand. When the weather is dry, the sand squeaks and seems to sing as you walk on it. The beach also has beautiful vistas, but limited parking and therefore limited crowds.

⚓

Beverly

EARLY SHIPS, RAGING RAILROADS

Beverly calls itself "The Birthplace of the American Navy," though some may dispute this title. The claim is that it produced the first ship commissioned by the United States military. That's kind of a stretch, because it was actually the American Army that used the ship since the American Navy did not yet exist in 1775.

The ship they built was the armed schooner *Hannah*. It was outfitted at Glover's Wharf, first sailing from Beverly Harbor on September 5, 1775. For this reason, Beverly believes it is America's naval birthplace. Among those who dispute the claim is the North Shore town of Marblehead. Nonetheless, such claims are difficult to dislodge, and an image of the *Hannah* can be found today stitched into the patch of the city's police department.

This all happened after the earthquake. But Beverly already had a history by that time. Beverly was originally part of the Naumkeag Territory and Salem, and was settled first by Roger Conant. However, the people of what would become Beverly, thought differently about religious matters than the people of Salem,

Singing Beach, Manchester-by-the-Sea, Mass

Walking on this beach under the right conditions produces a "singing" sound. *Postcard 1914.*

and especially Governor John Endicott. It may seem slight in retrospect, but even small variations of religious thought were significant in that day, and, as a result, Beverly grew into a separate community. It incorporated under its present name in 1668, being named after the Yorkshire (England) town of Beverley. The town is lucky to have a surviving dwelling from those early days—the 1679 Balch House, named for original settler John Balch.

Like most New England towns from that era, the village of Beverly gathered around its meetinghouse and followed the precept set by the General Court of Massachusetts, that called for all houses to be no more than a half mile away from it. This was generally for protection from possible attack, especially by Indians. Beverly also granted each of its families an acre of ground for farmland away from the village, and it laid out a common where livestock could feed. This was in the shape of a triangle, with streets and houses or buildings on each side.

After King Phillip's War (1675-1676), fears of Indian raids subsided and most tightly-knit villages gave way to towns that were more spread out. In Beverly, this led to the establishment of various neighborhoods, of which there are now twelve. Nonetheless, the period up to the American Revolution and the first decades of the 1800s were fairly stable in Beverly, and only changed when the railroad and the various waves of immigration brought change to all Boston-area towns.

In Beverly, like most of the region, the earliest immigrants were largely from Ireland and Italy, with some Russians and Swedes mixed in. These people came to North America because of poverty and social upheaval in their own lands Many settled in the Rantoul Street area, where factories were later built. Beginning in 1852, the street has been home to various ethnic groups. It is today part of Route 1A.

The street is named for Robert Rantoul, who bought land between Cabot Street and the railroad tracks in 1841. The railroad to Boston had just opened. Its station was located near the Essex Bridge over the Bass River.

Rantoul Street ran northwest from Cabot Street, then and now the major thoroughfare, at an acute angle. Much of the population lived on or near Cabot Street and people wanted the railroad station moved to Cabot Street. The railroad was finally able to persuade Rantoul to sell his land for that purpose.

The building of the station led to the location of businesses there, including a number of factories. These factories and the railroad brought jobs and immigrants. People from many ethnic backgrounds (mainly from northern and western Europe) moved to Rantoul Street and its surrounding areas. To help assimilate into the new surroundings, many ethnic groups set up their own organizations and stores. Credit unions, markets, restaurants, bakeries, and clothing shops all appeared and most were individualized for each ethnic group. Rantoul Street became a bustling location for immigrants and their families who worked in nearby factories.

The railroad also brought commuters who lived in neighboring towns, and wealthy Bostonians who wanted to spend their summers on Beverly's Gold Coast and farms. In some cases, families stayed all summer while fathers commuted to Boston to their businesses.

Rantoul Street served as the industrial area for the town until the building of the United Shoe Machinery factory ("The Shoe") on Elliot Street in 1906. This industrial growth had an early antecedent and in fact Beverly claims to be the birthplace of the American Industrial Revolution. That title is based on the fact that the first American cotton mill was built there. Beverly also has one of the first Sunday schools in the country, established in 1810. The town was incorporated as a city in 1894.

Roller Blading Down Factory Halls

THE "SHOE" IS SHED

Extending its industrial foundation, Beverly built something really big in 1902—a row of large factory buildings that stretched for a quarter of a mile. These buildings belonged to the United Shoe Machinery Corporation (USM). Known as "The Shoe," it has stood at that location since 1906, making machines that made shoes. It was built from reinforced concrete and held sway as the world's largest concrete building for thirty-five years, until surpassed by Boulder (later Hoover) Dam. It is, even today, considered one of the most significant industrial buildings in the country. It remained in operation until 1987.

When the United Shoe Machinery Company opened it doors in 1903, it created lots of new jobs. By 1920, nearly half of the people living in the factory's vicinity also worked there, including lots of immigrants. The Shoe took some civic responsibility when it paid for a public school for the children of its workers, one that remained until the year 2000. It also gave the town a recreation club, which became today's Beverly Golf and Tennis.

Its location additionally bore a historic note. The Shoe was built on a huge lot, the former Balch estate—250 acres that had been farms and houses, a mill, a wharf, some marshes, and rock ledges that were ground up to make cement from which the factory was fashioned. But it wasn't just the land on which the factory was built that involved United Shoe Machinery. Housing was built for employees and dams created ponds that could be used for recreation and fresh water. During the Second World War, victory gardens on factory property helped workers provide food for their families and to send some to American troops on the war fronts as well.

Activities to benefit workers and the community were a priority—agricultural fairs, garden competitions, a golf and tennis club (now a country club), fields for baseball games between workers and from the Bevery and Boston plants, and even boating clubs.

Although USM functioned essentially as a monopoly in its field until 1978, it also had a reputation as a benevolent employer and model member of the community.

Another aspect to the reign of The Shoe in Beverly was the positive effect it had on transportation in the region. The Eastern Railroad (whose tracks we'll cross again when we talk about Lynn) became part of the Boston & Maine Railroad, and its tracks ran right by the United Shoe property, enhancing and enabling commerce both there and in other towns.

By 1911, according to the old Massachusetts Bureau of Statistics, Beverly residents as a whole had higher annual earnings than the residents of any other city in the state. The company was a model employer. About 1909, the company initiated its own state-chartered industrial school, where generations of future workers and managers were trained. The newly formed Beverly Industrial School was "the first successful school for mechanics in the United States," according to *New England Magazine,* in 1911.

Among its 3,000 workers in Beverly by 1911, the company acknowledged about 100 female office workers and another 70 or 80 girls in the factory, according to a company brochure. They all "begin their work ten minutes later than the men and leave ten minutes earlier, so that a proper distance is maintained between the sexes as they enter and leave the factory," the brochure adds. This provides societal insight from 100 years ago.

The site's tidewater location made it a prominent point in Beverly history. The tidal basin, long dammed for industrial use, was the original landing place for Beverly's founding "planters." A bronze plaque set in a projecting boulder at the Upper Shoe Pond's north end commemorates the landing point of these town fathers. The path connecting the landing to the Balch House site (home of John Balch, one of Beverly's original settlers) is further identified by a bronze marker on a cut granite base at the site along Balch Street. The Friends Mill (c.1850), at the southwest corner of the site, replaced a much earlier mill and dam (c.1660). Throughout the property, a wide variety of artifacts is displayed, including refurbished antique USM equipment/machinery, dozens of wall-mounted vintage photo enlargements, and an original IBM time clock used at The Shoe in the early 1900s,

You'll learn more later about USM's template for successful sales of its equipment and about an intriguing individual who brought shoemaking machinery out of its homespun era, but for now you need to know that the company flourished for decades, finally declining and closing its Beverly doors in 1987. When they did, the factory became a 1.2 million square-foot white elephant. Nobody knew what to do with it; no one wanted to buy it. A lot of people had lost their livelihoods and no obvious replacement was on the horizon.

The decline had been gradual, stemming largely from the breakup of the company after the U.S. Supreme Court had declared it to be a monopoly in violation of the Sherman Ant-Trust Act. The company's subsidiaries failed in the main, and the Beverly Plant closed its doors in 1987. During the final years, the building itself had declined. A few companies now occupied the space, huddled closely together as if for protection. One CEO of a startup company that moved in during the year 1991, talked about what remained as long, dark corridors where it was now possible to ride a bike from one end of the building to another without so much as a speed bump. In its heyday, those same halls had echoed with the whirling sounds of secretaries and messengers roller-skating from one department to another over the long distances.

Black & Decker was the last owner, and their asking price, while steadily declining (like the building) was still too dear until, in 1995, they reached a price low enough that Cummings Properties was interested. The owners had realized the futility of paying to heat a building that brought little income, and spotting a "live one" in Cummings, sold it for half a million dollars, what the building had cost in 1902, and a bargain at less than a dollar per square foot.

Cummings Properties bought the complex in 1996. They developed it into a grouping of high-tech companies and medical offices called Cherry Hill Industrial Park, on the border with the town of Danvers. It houses numerous firms. Parker Brothers, maker of games like Monopoly, Risk, Ouija, and Clue, had offices in Beverly. It is now owned by Hasbro.

Beverly is also the home of the well-known Landmark School for students with learning disabilities.

But the purchase price bought nothing without the rehabilitation and additional expenses that went with it. It cost Cummngs $1 million to clean up pollution on the property and to rehab the building for use by technology companies and as office space. It also took six years and an eventual payout of $60 million. Imagine, if you can, installing 2,200 new windows, twenty-seven acres of roof, and miles of wiring, pipes, and carpet.

The cost was worth it. Hundreds of companies moved in: some retail, some biotech or software, paying rents of up to $21 per square foot, and forming by

Following spread:
A huge and active factory that employed thousands of North Shore workers, this plant continues to maintain an important presence in today's Beverly with its new technologies. *Courtesy of Cummings Properties.*

themselves what amounted to a small city with a wide variety of products and services, and bringing hundreds of millions of dollars of income to the area.

It seems historically fitting that the ancestor to the current head of the Cummings Properties goes back to 1636 in the settling of Beverly.

Like other Cape Ann towns, as mentioned earlier, Beverly has a history as a place of summer residence for those who could afford it. One such was President William Howard Taft, who rented a home, located where the Italian Garden is now in Lynch Park, in the summers of 1909 and 1910. He came back during his final two summers as President, but this time to Paramatta, which he rented from someone else. In fact, Beverly Hills, California, was named after Beverly Farms where Taft had vacationed.

As early as 1920, Beverly was becoming a suburban community. Those who didn't work at United Shoe commuted to Boston, about thirty to forty-five minutes away. This continued a sort of evolving trend of transition, where the town's development can be traced to the church and then the factory, and later to its attraction to vacationers and those who preferred and could afford suburban living.

What appeared to be a "white elephant" that would never move off the market, instead, became a triumph of capitalism with re-adaptive use. *Courtesy of Cummings Properties.*

Eleonora Sears

THE GOLD COAST'S GOLDEN SPORTSWOMAN

Eleonora Randolph Sears was a leading figure in Boston society early in the 20th century. She was not only a member of a leading Boston family, but she was perhaps the greatest woman athlete of her era, and she had a personality to match her backhand.

"Eleo," as she was known, had a Beverly association as well. Her family owned an estate on Paine Avenue, in Pride's Crossing, where there were many estates owned by wealthy families.

Her father was a shipping tycoon who had vast holdings of real estate and belonged to the top layer of society. His father, Richard Sears, had been a U.S. Open tennis champion. They were descendants of President Thomas Jefferson.

Eleo rode and bred horses, won a 1912 horse race in San Diego, took part in steeplechase, fielded a women's polo team in Monterey, and drove a coach down Fifth Avenue in New York to the amazement of other coachmen. (But she only did that on a bet.)

It was on her own that she invaded the polo field of the Burlingham Country Club, near San Francisco, and rode out to where the visiting British international team was practicing, asking if she could join them. She was not allowed, and nearly lost her club membership just for asking. Moreover, since she was wearing riding breeches and riding astride, rather than sidesaddle, a local mother's club wrote:

> Such unconventional trousers and clothes of the masculine sex are contrary to the hard and fast customs of our ancestors. It is immodest and wholly unbecoming a woman, having a bad effect on the sensibilities of our boys and girls.

Eleo was an excellent yachtsman as well, once beating Alfred Vanderbilt's yacht in a race. Vanderbilt would win the America's Cup three times. (She and Vanderbilt had a long relationship, thought to be romantic, but it did not end in marriage.)

At Newport, where she spent many summers, Eleo was the first person of either sex to swim the four-and-a-half miles from Bailey's Beach to First

Beach. Long distances were nothing new to her. She once walked from Newport to Boston in seventeen hours, and frequently walked from Boston to Providence. She could do that in less than ten hours.

Eleanora Sears was probably best known for her skill at tennis. She won the U.S. women's doubles championship four times, with two different partners, and mixed doubles once. Writers have said that she caused a scandal every time she stepped on a court. She certainly opened the sports world to women as no one had done before.

When she played squash for the first time in 1918, she beat the best male player in the club, and, at age 46, she won the first national women's squash title. Golf? She was outstanding; baseball, too. What about football? She was a fullback. She was great on the ice, as well, but not as a figure skater. She played hockey. She also boxed and was one of the best trap shooters in New England.

Eleo was an aviatrix, one of the first women to fly a plane. She also "flew" when she drove cars. She raced, and drove too fast on the public roads. She had a high-powered roadster in which she zoomed around the roads of Massachusetts. The police noticed this one summer, but they couldn't catch up with her to give her a ticket, so they had to go to her house to present it.

Her 240 athletic trophies show that she excelled in many sports, but she was also a great beauty, who had many boy friends and was completely immersed in the social life of the upper class, very popular in Boston and New York and often included on Best Dressed lists, such as in the year 1909, when she was known as the "Best-gowned woman in America."

The Prince of Wales, who later became King of England for a short spell, and then took on his lifetime identity as the Duke of Windsor, was on the top of every social list. In 1924, when he was at Myopia Hunt Club on the North Shore, he decided to attend a ball in Boston. Eleo lived in a townhouse on Beacon Street and attended the same ball. The Prince found her so fascinating that he danced all night with her. He later married another American, Wallis Simpson. Eleo remained unmarried.

The famous actress, Ethel Barrymore, (Drew is her great niece) wrote about a time she stayed with Eleo:

In the evenings at Beverly Farms when I had to stay indoors and play the piano for Mr. and Mrs. Sears, Eleo would be on the porch with a beau. I never knew anybody who had so many beaux and such nice ones, but she never married anybody.

Famed portraitist John Singer Sargent rendered this work at Pride's Crossing in 1921.
Eleo Sears was one of the greatest female athletes of her time, and a socialite as well.

John Singer Sargent was asked to sketch her, and did, in charcoal on paperboard. The sketch survives her, as does her home in Pride's Crossing, not far from the railway station. The station , too, still exists, but serves other functions.

⚓

Danvers

WITCH HYSTERIA, AN UNWILLING KING,

AND A HALF-LONG CARROT

The town that became Danvers was offered an early example of colonial resistance to royal authority. The town grew up along an Indian trail, left by the Naumkeag tribe, and was made into the Old Ipswich Road, a connector between Boston and Salem. The town was permanently settled as Salem Village, in 1636, and Salem Village petitioned the English monarch for a charter in order to become a town. Legend relates that the king would not sign the petition for a charter, but sent it back, scrawling instead the message, "The King Unwilling."

The town would not take "unwilling" as an answer, however, and in 1757, became a town in spite of the royal displeasure, making the king's message of refusal a part of the town seal, and naming the town "Danvers" for the Danvers Osborn family.

The royal decree may possibly not have made it across the Atlantic, but the town was in a snit about getting a charter in any case. It had waited over 100 years for incorporation, and it would have it. Why "Danvers"? And who was Danvers Osborne anyway? He was the man who had recently been made royal governor of New York, but had immediately taken his own life. Still, he was a British noble, and many towns were named for people of that ilk because it was believed that such deference would add influence. In any case, however the name was chosen, the show of independence was what really mattered.

Danvers, after all, had a little history it might rather forget. It was an earlier event, for which Danvers is best known: the Witch Hysteria of 1692 and the trials, some of which took place in Salem Village (later Danvers). This was something you might expect a town would want to forget about, but clearly Salem had made the most of it; and in Danvers, the house of Rebecca Nurse, a convicted witch, still stands as a historical landmark. During the witchcraft hysteria, Giles Corey became the only person pressed to death by stones. He and his wife are buried next to Crystal Lake.

As mentioned, Danvers was well-positioned between Boston and Salem and benefited from the roads and byways that were built between them. The railroad was such a byway, and it would come to Danvers, as would a street railway that was installed in 1884. At first it consisted of sixty-nine, horse-drawn trolleys, but the streetcars were later converted to electricity.

The town continues to have many farms, growing grains, vegetables and lots of fruit trees. The town has a river port known as Danvers-port, whose leading businesses are coal, wood, and lumber—primarily oak, pine, birch, maples and alder. A number of locations offer clay for making bricks and pottery, and the town's meadows offer peat, which can be used in place of coal for a cheap fuel. Its bricks became nationally known.

The town also grows a tart red fruit called the cowberry, which is something like a cranberry. Danvers is known for two breeds of vegetables that have originated there. One is the "Danvers onion," a medium-yellow vegetable with a small base and a narrow neck, with firm flesh. A section of Danvers is called "Oniontown" in its honor, but it is grown elsewhere from seeds. The other is the "Danvers Half-Long Carrot," introduced in the market gardens in 1871. It has a blocky top and reaches only six to seven and one-half inches in length. It is one of the best carrots for long-term storage.

Danvers had an important shoemaking industry from the late 19th into the 20th century, with successful companies like Ideal Baby Shoe. The industry continues at a section of town called the Plains, and there are also businesses in carpetmaking, flour mills, and iron works.

Danvers has had some significant and interesting buildings. Its Town Hall was built in 1855, and, though often modified and renovated, it still stands today. That same year, 1855, south Danvers became known as Peabody.

In 1878, the hauntingly remarkable Victorian Gothic-style Danvers State Hospital, also officially called an insane asylum and lunatic hospital, was built.

It is believed to have been the place where the pre-frontal lobotomy was first, unhappily, performed. A network of tunnels connected its buildings for use in inclement weather. The hospital closed in 1992. Most of it was demolished by 2006 and some apartment buildings meant to replace it were burned in a mysterious fire. Little remains of the complex today.

Fire and an explosion rocked the Arnel Company of Danvers in 2006, knocking homes off their foundations and shaking several North Shore towns, including Salem and Peabody. The company made inks and solvents. The cause of the blast was reported to be unintentional overnight heating of an ink-mixing tank containing flammable solvents. There were no fatalities.

This awe-inspiring Victorian edifice was a home for the mentally ill until destroyed for development. Photo from 1893. During the long and contested demolition, a mysterious fire razed nearly all of it in 2007.

⚓

Peabody

TANNER CITY

In days gone by—but not long ago—Peabody was the tanning center for the North Shore and beyond. All of the leather was tanned in Peabody and then much of it was shipped to neighboring Beverly. Tanning is the processing of leather to make it more durable and less likely to decompose. The process uses tannin, which comes from trees, especially oak. In fact, the name tannin comes from an old German word meaning "oak" or "fir" trees. Tanning also involves coloring the leather in most cases, and a tannery is where it all takes place.

Peabody's tanneries operated until the mid-20th century, then closed, but the names Leather City or Tanner City remain, and the high school teams are called the Tanners.

Peabody began as a farm town, with streams that allowed its residents to build mills and make use of their water power. Leather, of course, was primary among the industries. The town has subsequently become a middle-class suburb of Boston, with two large shopping malls in town and in Danvers. When the tanning firms closed, the city suffered economically at first, but has found replacement industries in the medical and technology companies located at Centennial Park.Early in the 20th century, the Corwin Manufacturing Company, which made automobiles during the brass era, (so-named for its brass fittings during the age of the horseless carriage and steam-powered vehicles) was located here.

Despite the residential boom and the industrial and commercial burgeoning, farming remains. Brooksby Farm, a working and historic farm managed by the city, occupies 275 acres, including a conservation area. Visitors can pick fruits, visit its farm stand or petting zoo and, in the winter, cross-country ski on its many trails. It is also the site of historic homes and the Woodland Garden.

The Salem Country Club, a private club located in Peabody, has a first-class golf course and has held major tournaments.

⚓

Salem

WITCHES AND MORE

Although it is often associated with it eighteenth-century witch trials, the history of Salem is far wider than that sorry episode. A major aspect of Salem history is its association with the sea and its era of international trade. That, too, is preserved in this city north of Boston. In fact, the Salem Maritime National Historic Site was the first such site named by Congress.

The village of Salem (originally "Naumkeag" after the resident Indian tribe) was founded at the mouth of the Naumkeag River by Roger Conant and other fishermen from Cape Ann, in 1626. The location had been a Native American village and trading post.

Three years later, it was renamed "Salem," an offshoot of the Hebrew and Arabic words meaning "peace." At that point, John Endicott arrived and was appointed governor by the Dorchester Company. Roger Conant vacated the land and was given a 200-acre grant for his graceful cooperation.

However, back in London, the newly-chartered Massachusetts Bay Company decided, after some disagreement, that John Winthrop would be governor instead and that Endicott would be his assistant. It was at this time that hundreds of mostly Puritans sailed for Massachusetts, landing first at Salem, but relocating the next year to Charlestown, and then moving across the river to Boston. This influx of people was part of the Great Migration, caused by religious disputes between the English King and the Puritans. It included many ministers and their followers, who would become religious leaders in coastal New England.

Conant built the first house in Salem on what is today Essex Street, almost opposite the Town Market. In 1639, he and others signed the building contract to enlarge the meetinghouse in Town House Square for the First Church in Salem. The city still owns the document he signed and keeps it at City Hall. Conant remained active in Salem throughout his life, dying at 87, in the year 1679.

When we think of Salem today, we envision the area that huddles close to the sea, but the original Salem was a lot bigger. It included a great deal of today's North Shore, inland as far as Middleton and Topsfield, and extended to Marblehead, parts of Beverly, Manchester-by-the-Sea, Wenham, and a section of Danvers.

Some people try to point out that Salem's witchcraft trials really took place in Salem Village, not in Salem, and therefore, in Danvers. That objection overlooks the fact that Salem Village was part of Salem at the time, so it's not a legitimate historical objection to the association of Salem with witchcraft. Salem gets most of the ink in connection with the witchcraft trials, and the best-known trials of 1692 were held there, but they were also held in Ipswich, Boston, and Charlestown.

Although many were accused of witchcraft and 150 were arrested and put in jail, most were not convicted. However, twenty-six were convicted in Salem in 1692. The next year, thirty-one arrests resulted in only three

The 1819 Custom House is part of the National Historic Site, and was the workplace of Nathaniel Hawthorne, whose birthplace is just up the street.

convictions. Of those convicted, nineteen were hanged and one refused to plea and was crushed to death with stones, which still did not result in a plea. This was the most violent of the deaths and received a lot of attention.

The case that began the "hysteria" also got a lot of attention, probably because it was the most interesting story. It happened in Salem Village in 1692. Two young girls, Betty Parris, age 9, and her cousin Abigail Williams, age 11, began to have "fits" that went beyond the epileptic ones that were known in those days. These girls were the daughter and niece of Rev. Samuel Parris, and that fact cannot be overlooked. The girls screamed, threw things, crawled under furniture, and twisted themselves into strange positions. They said they were being stuck with pins and pinched. A doctor who examined them could find no cause for their behavior or any illness. Soon this behavior "spread" to other girls.

Those accused and convicted of afflicting these girls were minorities and outcasts, who had no means of defending themselves. Sarah Good was a homeless woman, an indigent taken to begging for food and shelter. No one defended her. Even her 4-year-old daughter accused her. Sarah Osborne had committed the sin of staying away from church. She rarely attended. More than that, she was believed to have had sexual relations with an indentured servant.

Tituba was a slave who had told fascinating stories to the children. When questioned, she told even wilder stories, confessed to witchcraft and riding brooms, and named others who were witches. Despite all this, perhaps the wildest and least explained part of the tale is that Tituba was not tried or hanged for her supposed crimes. She was released from jail and disappeared.

It all makes a good story, particularly in retrospect. Over time, the hysteria seems to have run its course, and the trials and accusations ended, but Salem has never lost (and probably doesn't want to lose) its reputation as a center for witchcraft and witchcraft trials. These days it capitalizes on this reputation.

But Salem has other history, too—not just a separate and bizarre (if entertaining) event, but history that affected the rest of the nation.

The British Back Down

Colonel David Mason received a commission from the Massachusetts Committee of Safety, in November of 1774, as an artillery officer, a position for which he had experience fighting in the French and Indian War at Ft. William Henry, and fortifying Boston. The man was self-taught, interested in science and something of an inventor. In fact, he had even discussed electricity with none other than Benjamin Franklin.

At the time of the conflict with Britain, David Mason had seventeen French 12-pounder cannons, and was refitting them and mounting them onto carriages in Salem. This was at the time when General Gage, the British governor of Massachusetts, was attempting to crush any incipient rebellion by confiscating arms and ammunition from potential rebels. Colonel Mason's seventeen cannons certainly fit that description.

It would have been good to keep the cannons a secret from Gage, but he was too clever for that. Gage had spies all over the place, just as the colonials did, and sure enough, one of them had uncovered the secret Salem guns and had run to Gage to sell this juicy information for a handsome fee. Gage was glad to get it and planned to get the guns, too.

He immediately decided to send troops to find these guns and take or destroy them. He needed a reliable commander for this mission, and his choice was Colonel (the Honorable) Alexander Leslie, age 44, the son of an earl, a member of the military since 1753, and for the past nine years in command of the 64th regiment. Leslie was one of Gage's most trusted assistants, a man whom Gage frequently consulted about the defense of Boston.

Leslie was, in fact, one of the best British officers in North America, and he would go on to serve with distinction during the Revolution, rising to become a Brigadier General during that conflict and later reaching the rank of Lieutenant General. But, like many British officers during the early part of the Revolution in Boston, Leslie would not cover himself in glory during this Salem raid. The British would find few heroes among its officer ranks while they were in Boston.

Leslie was a logical choice, and it was he who led the 240 troops of his 64th Regiment as they set sail, on February 26, 1775, from Castle William (on Castle Island) in Boston Harbor. They reached Marblehead Harbor in a short time and disembarked, intending to march from there to Salem. These were small towns without many people, and Leslie expected most of them would be inside the meetinghouse, since it was a Sunday afternoon. He hoped to make the march without stirring up too much attention. It was a rational idea, but it didn't work out because the mariners of Marblehead couldn't afford to spend a Sunday in church. These men were fishers of fish and had to eke out a living, Sabbath or not.

When Leslie's troops landed between 2 p.m. and 3 p.m., at Homan's Cove on Marblehead Neck, the people of Marblehead knew immediately what they were up to, and they sent an alarm at once to Salem—a rider actually passed the troops. A Tory told Leslie to search a certain blacksmith's shop on the other side of the bridge. Meanwhile, in Salem, the townsfolk were, indeed, in the meetinghouse. But they would not remain there for long.

In Salem, residents beat a tattoo on their drums, just outside the church, while others yelled out, "The foe, the foe, they come!" Colonel Leslie's soldiers, professional and seemingly unperturbed, continued their march in single file. Now that the jig was up, their fife and drum corps played "Yankee Doodle," as an in-your-face insult to the townfolk. It was a tune the colonials hated, since its words belittled them. The British arrogantly marched and played all the way to North Bridge. Then they halted. They had to.

The drawbridge was open from the opposite side and some of the planks had been removed. On the other side of the bridge, stubborn and resolute-looking citizens of Salem faced them in surly stance. His lieutenants urged Leslie to fire upon the crowd. But Leslie had a cooler head. Perhaps he recalled the Boston Massacre of a few years back when British soldiers had fired into a crowd with a negative result for themselves. He may not have wanted to start a war, or he may have listened to Captain John Felt, a colonial militiaman, who shouted at Leslie in a loud voice that had to be heard by everyone within range: "If you do fire, you will all be dead men!"

Better to find boats and ferry his men across, Leslie may have thought. There were boats along the side of the river, but the Americans got to them first and poked holes in them so that they could not be used. Leslie's squad of redcoats, angered by this action rushed them, threatening Joseph Whicher, who was doing some of the scuttling. As the British approached with bristling bayonets, Whicher dared them to run him through. One did get close enough to stick him and draw blood, but, in a close call, Leslie was able to restore order.

The number of colonials was growing, of course, as the word fanned out to neighboring towns, and militias and individuals hurried to Salem. Whatever cannons may have been hidden in that area had by now been removed to safer warrens. From Leslie's point of view, his hopes of a quiet seizure had been replaced by a likely disgrace.

The standoff was resolved by the minister of the First Church in Salem, Thomas Barnard, who had been a Tory, but was now a patriot. Realizing that Leslie did not want a war-starting "incident," the pastor suggested a face-saving compromise. Leslie's orders required him to search on the north side of the bridge. It would be lowered, and Leslie could march his soldiers fifty rods past the bridge if he agreed to immediately return to his ship. That's what happened. Bloodshed was averted, or at least postponed. The British returned to Boston without the cannons, but it had become clear to them that the Americans were ready for a fight, which could begin at any time.

Of course, it did start two months later, and Salem became a center for privateering. At war's end, it would become a major trading center, and, by 1790, Salem was the sixth largest city in the country. It's reputation in the China trade became known around the world.

"Leslie's Retreat" is today the name of a dog park and a restaurant in Salem. The events never quite got the attention they might have, and the British officer went on to serve the army well during the Revolution. *Leslie's Retreat at the NorthBridge on Sunday Feb'y 26, 1775* by Charles M. Endicott, 1856, Ives and Pease Printers.

Those codfish, caught off the banks, became a staple of trade with the West Indies and Europe. From the West Indies came sugar and molasses, while tea was imported from China and pepper from Sumatra in the East Indies. In addition, ships from Salem visited Africa, Russia, Japan, and Australia.

At the turn of the century, international trade brought more profits to Salem, and during this Federalist period, many fine buildings and houses were built, including some by architect Samuel McIntire, who designed several Federalist mansions that stand today, many of them in the area around Chestnut Street. Today, a historic district is named for McIntire.

All things nautical thrived in Salem. Its homegrown mariner, Nathaniel Bowditch, revolutionized navigation with his publishing of the first edition of *American Practical Navigator,* in 1802. Bowditch became known as the founder of modern maritime navigation, and his book continued to be popular until the end of the 19th century; it was considered the bible of sea navigation.

Trade Blockade

Trade prospered in Salem until, by 1810, its port was providing five percent of all the income in the country. It had fifty-plus wharves with warehouses attached, and it traded with nations around the world, bringing in coffee, tea, cotton, silk, spices, molasses, and porcelain. In many cases, the wily merchants of Salem allowed their trusted captains a free hand to set sail with a cargo and to bring home the best cargo they could find. Giving them this free hand ultimately took ships farther and farther from home.

The port of Salem had shops, like the West India Goods and Grocery Store that sold imported goods that were hard to get anywhere else. What they sold depended on what cargo had been landed that week or that day; but whatever it was, it would be exciting. People from around New England came to shop.

But this golden age of trade would not last. During that first decade of the 19th century, troubles were brewing with England and France, problems that interfered with American trade and made it dangerous for her sailors. France engaged in unfair trade practices and sometimes confiscated American ships. The British Navy, at war with the France of Napoleon, was stretched thin for manpower on its ships, so it used press gangs which would go into seashore taverns and even on board foreign ships, forcing sailors to join their navy, even native-born Americans.

Britain was also curtailing the rights of neutrals (mostly Americans) from trading with Europe, while France was controlled by Napoleon.

President Jefferson reacted, in 1807, by having Congress impose an embargo banning trade into and out of the United States. Not only did it fail, but it was also very unpopular, especially in New England, which, of course, depended on foreign trade.

Meanwhile, the naval conflict had a salubrious effect upon the U.S. Navy, which performed far beyond expectations. The American navy, which Congress had commissioned in 1794 with six original vessels, began the war with nine frigates and eight smaller vessels. The British had 1,048 vessels of all kinds. But in the first few months of war, before the British managed to effectively blockade American ports, the tiny U.S. Navy achieved spectacular results.

From the start of the war in June through the rest of the year 1812, American ships captured hundreds of British merchant ships. The *London Times* asked, "Good God! Can such things be?" And the *Pilot* fretted about the notices on *Lloyd's List* that showed "…upward of five hundred British vessels captured in seven months.…Five hundred merchantmen and three frigates! Can these statements be true? Anyone who had predicted such a result of an American war this time last year would have been treated as a madman or a traitor.…"

Part of this was the splendid acquittal of the U.S. naval frigates. In that period, *Essex* took 11 merchantmen, *Constitution* nine, *President* seven, and *Argus* six. But privateers, many of them from Salem, did frightful damage. English merchants in the West Indies complained to parliament that Americans were invading harbors protected with batteries and that they had taken 200 merchantmen, carried off cattle, and even blockaded Jamaica. Privateers exacted a price on British shipping that it could scarcely afford. The British sent warships to rid these harbors of privateers, but then had trouble catching them.

By 1813, however, frigates of the British Navy were patrolling outside harbors along Massachusetts Bay. Though they were largely successful in their mission, one ship, H.H.S. *Nymphe* was driven from the waters off Rockport by local citizens in the Battle of Sea Fencibles.

Another battle southeast of Cape Ann between the U.S. frigate *Chesapeake* and H.M.S. *Shannon,* on June 1, 1813, resulted in a British victory, but a memorable slogan. The American captain, James Lawrence, had a chance to take the British ship *Shannon,* but instead, brought his ship alongside, and in the ensuing battle, the British guns crippled the American vessel and killed Captain Lawrence. His final order was "Don't give up the ship!" which became the motto of the U.S. Navy. In fact, the *Chesapeake* was given up after a fifteen-minute battle and many casualties on both sides.

Maintaining a blockade was not easy. It took fully armed ships and crews to do it and they had to stay outside harbors for long periods at a time. Even then, darkness, fog, or lack of concentration allowed some of the fastest American vessels to escape. When the blockading ships went after them, the port was unattended and other ships could slip out. Finally, the British ships arranged to work in pairs.

At this point, the privateers moved to the other side of the Atlantic ocean and began attacking vessels off the coast of Britain and Ireland. Few of them were ever caught because they were built to outrun armed vessels. One of them, the *Governor Tompkins,* sailed right in among British ships of a protected convoy and took three prizes. Another, the *Kemp,* saw an escorted convoy with seven merchant vessels, drew the frigate that was protecting them into a wild goose chase, and scurried back quickly to take five of the merchant ships as prizes.

They also took mail packets regularly in the Irish Sea, and some privateers sailed right up the Thames River, dashing past armed warships. One British ship reported sighting ten American vessels in a voyage between Britain and Spain. One schooner, chased out of the West Indies by a British frigate, showed up next in the English Channel where it took twenty merchantmen. The captain sent a ship back to London with a message for Lloyd's (the Scottish insuring company):

> all the ports, harbors, bays, creeks, rivers, inlets outlets, islands, and seacoast of the United Kingdom of Great Britain and Ireland in a state of strict and rigorous blockade.

It may have been a bluff, but insurance premiums soared. Those in Glasgow declared:

the number of American privateers with which our channels are infested, the audacity with which they have approached our coasts, have proved ruinous to our commerce, humbling to our pride, and discreditable to the British navy; that 800 vessels have been taken by that Power, whose maritime strength we have impolitically held in contempt, and that there is reason to anticipate still more serious suffering.

"Audacity" was the right word. One American ship had sailed its prizes to China and auctioned them there. Another captured a ship with 20,000 pounds of gold dust and a fortune in opium aboard. One captured a ship bearing uniforms for the Duke of Wellington's army. English markets ran out of fish because so few trawlers were available. The admiralty warned ships from sailing the coast from Bristol to Portsmouth without an armed escort.

The Americans, meanwhile, were doing poorly in Canada and the British had burned Washington, D.C. Soon, both sides were eager to end the war that nobody really wanted in the first place.

The war was especially unpopular in New England and among the Federalist Party members, who were particularly strong in Salem and on the North Shore. The New England economy was highly dependent on trade, and the British blockade threatened to destroy it entirely. The Federalists saw it as costly, unlikely to end well, and wanted to end it. They not only spoke and wrote against it, but also would, toward the end, take action against it.

It took until 1814 for the British blockade of New England seaports to have a serious effect. At that point, the Federalists of New England sent delegates to the Hartford Convention in December 1814, which went so far as to discuss seceding from the union. They settled for proposed Constitutional amendments that would have answered their grievances. Moreover, Massachusetts was ready to make a separate peace with England. None of that would happen. Before the proposals could be presented, Andrew Jackson smashed the British in the Battle of New Orleans, and a peace treaty had already been signed.

In December 1814, the Treaty of Ghent returned things to their pre-war status. Impressment of seamen, which had been a major cause of the war, was not mentioned. The Battle of New Orleans, won by Andrew Jackson weeks later, came after peace had been settled.

The privateers, among them those from Salem, had earned perhaps $30 million for their efforts, although much of the domestic shipping fleet would have to be replaced. This war marked the beginning of decline for the port, which had been the leading port in America up to then. Salem's harbor was too small and too shallow to compete with Boston, Baltimore, and Philadelphia, or especially with New York, which would soon connect with the Midwest via the Erie Canal.

Salem's growth, however, continued in other ways. Salem is filled with excellent architecture from this period, much of it attributable to the China Trade, but even this trade would die out.

The Derby Family

The Derbys of Salem were a family of super-achievers whose exploits paralleled those of Salem—or perhaps the other way around. They played a major role in Salem history and even had an influence on American history. The patriarch of the family was Richard Derby (1712-1783), master and owner of sailing vessels that plied the world's oceans, bringing wealth to himself, his family, and Salem. In 1757, when he retired from sailing, two of his sons, John and Richard, took over his vessels. Another of his sons, Elias Hasket Derby, later known as "King Derby," became business head of the firm. Elias Hasket Derby's title of "King Derby" was given to him by author Nathaniel Hawthorne in his book, *The Scarlet Letter*.

Richard, the father, served as a member of the general court of Massachusetts and outfitted privateers to attack British shipping, just as the British had done to Salem in 1776. His second wife, Sarah Langley Hersey, of Hingham, used the fortune that he left her in part to found the Derby Academy in Hingham.

His son, Elias Derby, an outstanding accountant, learned the mercantile trade and had ships trading in the English and French islands. He also made improvements in shipbuilding, and during the Revolutionary War lent the government many supplies for the army and boats for the use of troops, furnished coal for the French fleet, and became a leader in building a frigate for the new country. He also took a large hand in furnishing privateers to prey on British shipping (Salem equipped 158 armed vessels in all during the War of 1812.)

Richard's oldest son, Richard Jr., was an active patriot, serving as a delegate, in 1774, to the Ipswich Convention.

The youngest son, John Derby, owned the ship *Columbia*, and discovered the river, known today by that name, on its second voyage. Richard took word of the Battles of Lexington and Concord to England on his brother John's fast ship, *Quero*.

After the battle, it became clear that patriots knew that General Gage would be sending his version of the fighting (including his point of view of who was at fault at Lexington) to put the best spin on it for British consumption. The Americans were on to him. They put together testimonials from people on both sides who had witnessed the events, and asked Richard Derby to get it to England as fast as possible.

The *Lively*, the ship Gage had dispatched, had a four-day head start, but *Quero* was not only fast, it was piled high with sail to make it even speedier. In addition to letters and documents, Derby carried copies of the *Salem Gazette*, which had a detailed account of the events of April 19th. Although the British had a ship blocking Salem harbor, the schooner managed to slip by and move out to sea. The sailors had no idea where they were going or why, until they reached Newfoundland where it became obvious that their port of call would be in London.

A busy, though shallow harbor when ships of the house of Derby plied the seas as far as China, this scene has glimpses of many things that took place on a daily basis just across from the Custom House and the Derby House. *Salem, Mass shipping in the 1770s*. Leizelt, Balthasar Friedrich, engraver, 1777.

On May 27th, the *Quero* weighed anchor off the Isle of Wight in the British Channel, a very fast passage of only twenty-nine days. Derby quickly got his materials to Arthur Lee, who was working with Ben Franklin. Lee got everything printed and to the right sources, and soon, all of London was abuzz with the news that British citizens in America had been fired on by His Majesty's troops.

People were aghast, and when they asked those in the government about it, they were assured that the accounts were erroneous and that the official report would be forthcoming. It was, in time. But having heard the American account, with its sworn statements from many sources, the report of a general in the field was less believable. The Americans had won the public relations race.

Having taken the pulse of the public reaction in Britain, Derby sailed quickly home. When his ship got to Salem, however, he wasn't on board. He had slipped ashore somewhere else on the American coast. Whether it was Quincy or Dorchester or elsewhere isn't known, but his destination is known. He headed right to Cambridge and General Washington to let him know that the American side had arrived first and had met the better reception, bringing sympathy for the American cause.

The story of Derby's fast ships didn't end there, however. At the end of the war, it was a Derby ship that brought the first news from France that the peace treaty had been signed in Paris.

"King" Derby continued to expand the family business, opening trade to St. Petersburg, Russia, in 1784, and sending ships on 125 voyages all over the world. This included the East Indies and beginning regular trade with India in 1791, thereby earning Derby the name "Father of American Commerce with India" and being the first to hoist an American flag outside Calcutta. Also, his ship, *Grand Turk*, was the first American ship to trade with China.

However, the China trade showed a profit for only a few years and then the market became glutted with tea. Those trips were expensive and, inevitably, trade with China fell off. Derby ships spent more time in Mauritius and sailed on from there to other ports.

By 1790, Salem was the sixth largest town in America, and, in 1798, Derby contributed $10,000 of the $75,000 given by private citizens to help start a U.S. Navy. The navy began on the advice of King Derby to President John Adams and the Congress, which authorized acceptance of vessels that citizens had built for national service. At his death, King Derby left an estate of over $1 million, the largest in the nation at that point.

Derby's sons added to the family wealth. Elias Junior made important voyages to France and Naples, and also found some merino sheep dislocated by war that he brought to America. During the War of 1812, he built the first broadcloth loom in Massachusetts. The King's children completed Derby Wharf, extending it 2,000 feet into the harbor.

Peabody-Essex Museum

Peabody-Essex Museum, or PEM, as it is called, is an outstanding museum, located in the heart of Salem, whose major collections are tied to the China Trade that was so big in Salem in the 18th and 19th centuries. A group of sea captains and traders met in 1799 to form the East India Marine

The Peabody-Essex Museum houses one of the largest and best collections of Asian art and historical pieces, as well as maritime art. It owns twenty-four historical structures, many near the museum. This is now part of one of the oldest museums in the country. *Photo: Detroit Publishing, 1910.*

Society, which later became known as the Peabody Museum. The society required its members to collect items, which it termed "natural and artificial curiosities" especially from Asia and the Pacific regions. They collected some rare items, both in age and provenance (ownership history).

Next door to the Peabody Museum was the Essex Institute, whose collections in East India Marine Hall were complemented by a library in Plummer Hall. The institute also had educational programs and owned two historical houses, built by Samuel McIntire during the Federal Period, which were open to the public. In 1992, the two museums merged to form the Peabody-Essex Museum, and in 2003, PEM opened a new wing that doubled its exhibition space, allowing it to display items previously in storage. Among its present displays are the 19th-century Yin Yu Tang House, brought from China and reassembled, and many examples of maritime, Asian, and Oceanic art. It also owns twenty-four historic buildings and gardens, some in the galleries, but many lining the streets of Salem.

Hawthorne Made History Live

ON THE NORTH SHORE

Some American writers of fiction are renowned in large part for what they have brought to a particular time in our cultural or political history. Some have brought to life a specific time and region. They've allowed readers to imagine what it would have been like to live in a different time and place. Mark Twain, Washington Irving, James Fenimore Cooper, and Nathaniel Hawthorne were some who did this.

Nathaniel Hawthorne brought to life the days of the Puritans, with his moral allegories and his dark romantic novels, including *The Scarlet Letter*. He similarly brought to life Salem of the Federalist period, with overtones of the witchcraft heritage in his book *The House of Seven Gables*. The themes of Hawthorne's work are often moral allegories that follow Puritan thought and center on sin and the inherent evil of humanity.

His work was typically about New England and often set in Salem, where he lived part of his life. His family name was in fact "Hathorne," but he had it changed because an ancestor of that name presided over the witchcraft trials.

He was fascinated with the history of Salem, as well as its people, but he also hated the town, partly from a stultifying stint he had in a political appointment at Salem's customs house, where he held a three-year term before being bounced when the politics of the place changed. He also thought it a sleepy, dull town living on its past glories.

Hawthorne wrote *The Scarlet Letter* in 1850, when it became one of the first mass-produced books in America and an instant hit. Its early sales were immense for a novel of that day, with 2,400 books sold in the first ten days. It became an immediate best-seller.

The Scarlet Letter is the tale of the public shaming of Hester Prynne, who committed adultery with the minister, Rev. Arthur Dimmesdale (the reverend suffered profound guilt as a result of their affair), and the vengeance sought by Hester's husband. The theme of a romantic triangle or an illicit love affair was nothing new, but the steeping of the tale in Puritan morality and hypocrisy gave it added dimension. Some have called it the first true American novel.

Hawthorne followed it, in 1852, with *The House of Seven Gables*, a novel contemporary to his time, since it was set in the mid-19th century. He even used (as a background) the home owned by his cousin, not far from his own birthplace. This haunting tale was fraught with fraud, accusations of witchcraft and unexpected death, all of which recalls that the author himself often felt guilt-ridden by the involvement of his ancestors in the Salem witchcraft trials. More explicitly, the Pyncheon family featured in the novel, have built their fortune and even their house on dishonest shorings. In the preface to the book, Hawthorne makes clear its moral: "The wrongdoing of one generation lives into the successive ones and becomes a pure and uncontrollable mischief."

Artifacts of that era remain in the Salem of today. A ship replica that is open to visitors, the schooner *Fame of Salem*, is a tribute to the successful

This house is just down the street from Hawthorne's and was owned by his cousin and visited by the author as a boy. It may have been the inspiration for his Gothic novel years later, *The House of Seven Gables*. It is now a museum with secret passages. *Photo: Detroit Publishing, 1915.*

privateers in Salem from the War of 1812. The original ship was a fast Chebacco fishing schooner. It was converted into a privateer during that war and captured twenty prizes (probably including the first taken by an American ship) before she was wrecked in the Bay of Fundy in 1814.

Salem also considers itself the birthplace of the National Guard, because the first military muster was held on its common in the first decade. The muster stemmed from England's method to determine how many men were available for service. You "passed muster" when an inspection was successful.

In 1836, the town of Salem became a city, and in 1858, an amusement park was built at Salem Willows. In the last quarter of the 19th century, technology and invention became big in America, especially around Boston where Alexander Graham Bell lived, worked, and made history with his invention of the telephone with his partner, Salem-born Thomas A. Watson.

Tom Watson of Telephone Fame

Thomas Watson had a *rags-to-riches* story, but not in the economic sense. As a boy, he had enough to eat, clothes to wear, and a roof over his head that didn't leak. But he rose culturally to high society, and that takes some doing.

His father managed a large livery stable in Salem. Tom lived on the top floor of a house on the property, a house that was stuffed with stuff. They stored blankets and saddles and all kinds of horsey supplies on the bottom floor—lots of them.

The top floor was teeming with family, and Tom had regular chores, that included hauling all the fuel and every drop of water up two flights of stairs from a damp and dusky cellar. This wasn't lace-curtain Salem. The Watsons ate meals with their hands, helped by a knife that was used to steer the food into their mouths. If Tom even saw a fork, it only had two tines, like the ones a cook might stab a potato with, as was the style in his day.

Christmas and winter weekends were special for Tom. His father provided sleigh rides for the folks of Salem. Tom went too, sitting up front with his father, as he drove the horses o'er the fields of snow, laughing all the way, though the laughter probably came from their passengers who were tucked warmly beneath robes and blankets the Watsons kept on the first floor of the house.

Tom liked riding up there in plain sight as people heard the jingling bells and stopped to wave to the party. In a way, he was on display. And, you know, if you think of it, this sleigh riding was a sort of foreshadowing—an early sign that Tom would share his glory, most of the time, with at least one other person. Tom was riding up top, but Papa was top banana.

Here's another contradiction: In time, Tom would become an educational leader, but his own formal education was limited. If he presented his resume today businesses would probably put him to work bagging groceries or pricing products. It wouldn't matter; he'd probably wind up managing the store anyway. Managing was just something he did.

Between the ages of 6 and 14, he went to four different schools and always stood second in his class. That was okay with him. He liked that second spot, standing back in the shadow of someone else. He actually said he liked it because the first-ranking student always got called on to recite whenever the teacher wanted to impress a visitor. Tom, at this time, was shy; and that would shape his future.

Tom Watson didn't think much of the education Salem gave him. He learned to read quickly, but was not taught to read aloud with expression. He was good at math, but the schools didn't give him practical problems to solve. Tom liked practical problems.

Even at age 14, he thought about educational issues. He wondered why the schools taught history out of a book, especially in Salem where they had all those historical houses and ships and museums. And why didn't they use the ocean and the islands and the landforms to teach geography? He decided he could learn better by himself.

The reason he could read quickly was because he had taught himself to do so. His family owned one book—*Robinson Crusoe*—so he read that until the pages fell out. Salem didn't have a public library, but Tom got books cheaply anyway. There was a store that would rent a novel for two cents a day. Tom waited until Saturday to rent a book. Then he would speed read it over the weekend and return it Monday morning for just the two cents charge. He was thrifty, too, you see.

His grammar school had taught public speaking. They called it declaiming. Tom had to get up in front of the other boys and speak. But when he reached age 14, his first year of high school, the principal decided the students had to declaim in front of both boys and girls. For Tom, who was shy, this was too much. His parents let him quit the school.

He didn't quit declaiming, though. He began to take walks by himself in nature and he declaimed to the trees and the animals and the birds. He used poems or stories that he had memorized. He also tried to imitate the speaking methods of people he thought were good speakers. And he got quite good at it.

When he left school, he went to work, beginning at the bottom of the ladder, but he worked his way up quickly, taking courses at a school in Boston, where he learned bookkeeping, commercial law, and banking. He became a cashier, bookkeeper, and salesman, and even tried being a carpenter. He stayed in each job just long enough to know he didn't like the work, or that it wasn't challenging enough. He moved on quickly, like a boy skipping across stones in a brook without really getting his feet wet.

His first somewhat permanent job was in a machine shop. It was one of the best in the country and was located in Boston, near the present Government Center on Court Street. His boss was Charles Williams, who paid him the lordly sum of $3 a week. But he saved his money and by the time he started with Williams in 1872, he had already saved $240 and reckoned that he could retire with what he would earn by age 50 and live off the interest.

At the Williams shop, Tom Watson worked with electricity, which was little more than a curiosity in those days. A man named Thomas Edison had worked at this shop just before Tom got there. Edison hadn't even invented his electric light bulb then. It would be seven more years before he made the first practical electric light bulb, and a full decade before Edison would light just a section of New York City. And as for Boston—well, when Tom Watson walked home from his job, his path was lit by the flickering flames of gaslights.

Williams' workers did make electric fire alarms. One of the first and finest fire alarm makers was Moses Farmer, who also lived in Salem and lit his house with electric lights long before Edison invented his own. Farmer had recently installed Boston's fire alarm system, and he'd soon have Watson making his alarms at the Williams shop.

Four months later, Farmer's alarms got the supreme test when the Great Fire swept through much of downtown Boston. The fire stopped just before it got to the Williams shop, down the hill at the Old State House.

Tom Watson liked the work at Williams' shop, except when it became repetitive. Tom did not like boring, and at times like that, he recalled how his overworked mother made her tasks at home easier and quicker by using shortcuts and routines.

Tom tore a page from her book. He figured out ways to do the work in as few motions as possible and to move smoothly from one process into the next. Using the same sequence again and again, the work became automatic and fast. Without knowing it, he had done an early time-and-motion study.

He also invented special tools to improve and speed up his work. He used speed-reading to find out what had already been invented. Most fellow workers didn't know these things, but Tom was out to save time and effort. He didn't re-invent too many wheels in his time.

His boss, Charles Williams, noticed Tom's methods, and soon Tom was the top man in the shop. He worked so fast and so cleverly that he was never laid off even when hard times fell. Instead, when someone came in with only an idea of what they wanted and no idea of how it should look, Williams turned it over to Watson. Tom became known as a man who could make anything. He even found poetry in this work:

> I often felt an exaltation in my work akin to the ecstasies of my lonely walks," he recalled. "In the woods, I felt myself a living part of all creation. Now I thrilled with the knowledge that I myself was creating as I made stubborn metal do my will and take the shape necessary to enable it to do its allotted work. I should have been surprised then if any one had called those moments poetic but I know now there was some noble poetry in my life at Williams' shop.

As it happened, Tom was the right man at the right time. The decades that followed the Civil War would see a great surge of inventions, and during that period, being an inventor bore a great cachet. Inventors were the superstars of the era. Americans were beginning to believe that science was a solution to their sighs and sadnesses, and that inventors were the special people who would make their lives easier.

Electricity, like today's Internet and hand-held devices, attracted young people. Tom was young, and he had what it took to make inventors look good. Many inventors were not practical men. They had ideas, but didn't have the mechanical skills to put them in play. They needed someone else to put their plans into action. So a place like the Williams shop was a mechanical nirvana. Here, the so-called inventors could just deposit their ideas and Tom could build the machinery required to test their ideas.

This Salem boy, Tom Edison, became the partner of Alexander Graham Bell in the invention of the telephone and was founder of the world's largest shipyard in Braintree/Quincy.

Tom was good and he was fast, and these men needed both because inventors often had financial backers (or angels) who wanted results as quickly and cheaply as possible, so they could realize a return on their investments

By the beginning of 1874, Watson was the star of the Williams shop and inventors had begun to ask for him by name. Watson tells about one of these pre-occupied men:

> One day early in 1874 when I was hard at work for Mister Farmer (inventor of a fire alarm)...there came rushing out of the office door and through the shop to my work bench a tall, slender, quick-motioned young man with a pale face, black side-whiskers and drooping mustache, big nose, and high, sloping forehead crowned with bushy jet-black hair. It was Alexander Graham Bell, a young professor in Boston University, whom I then saw for the first time.

It was an auspicious meeting, one that would lead to the invention of the telephone. After that, Watson would become wealthy and go into another business. He opened the world's largest shipyard, which became the Fore River Shipyard in Quincy. They made mostly warships.

When shipping declined in Salem during the 19th century, it was replaced by manufacturing and commerce. Industries included tanneries, shoe factories, and the Naumkeag Steam Cotton Company.

The Great Salem Fire of 1914 began in the Korn Leather Factory and devastated the city, burning over 400 homes and leaving 3,500 families homeless. But while one part of the city was destroyed, the historical areas around Chestnut Street and the City Hall were not.

The historical and architectural treasures that remained allowed Salem to develop a new industry—tourism. Salem can also boast the country's first living-history museum, Pioneer Village, established in 1930. It is a recreated Puritan village that allows visitors to take part in activities common to a village of the Puritan era.

The oldest surviving structure in the city is Old Town Hall, built in 1816 on land donated by John Derby III and Benjamin Pickman, Jr. It served for thirty years as town hall until the new one was built on Washington Street.

⚓

Marblehead

FISHING BOATS AND RACING YACHTS

In Marblehead, one doesn't just reflect on the town's historic past—they live it every day.

Town Website

Call it unique, picturesque, cussed, distinctive, pixilated, fascinating—that's Marblehead, a town in love with liberty and rugged individualism. Its people and history, its crooked lanes and irregular houses, its customs and humor defy conformity and dullness. The irreligious settlers, the adventurous fishermen, the zealous patriots of 1776, the daring privateers of 1812, the clipper ship captains and yesteryear's fish peddlers imbued their town with a spirit as hardy as the rocky peninsula itself.

Priscilla Sawyer Lord and Virginia Clegg Gamage

Marblehead—The Spirit of '76 Lives Here

Marblehead—The Spirit of '76 Lives Here best describes Marblehead and its inhabitants, both past and present.

Members of the indigenous Naumkeag Tribe, familiar throughout this area, lived here under the leadership of their sachem, or chief, Nanepashemet. They called the place Massebequash. But by the time the first English settlers arrived, the numbers of that tribe were greatly reduced by disease.

The English settlers came from nearby Salem, of which the area was a part. The first of them probably arrived around 1629, but the date and identity of those who came are in doubt. Those who came had been dissatisfied by the strictness of the Puritans' customs and way of worshiping. So they went farther afield to Marblehead, where they got along well with the remaining Naumkeags. They were fishermen, a feisty group of pioneers standing up to the Puritan hierarchy as an indication of their continuing desire for liberty.

If sturdiness was a requirement, then the man who tradition calls the first settler, had that in spades. He was called Doliber, first name uncertain and his descendants were many. He settled on (what is now) Peach's Point, around Little Harbor, where he used a large, wooden barrel, called a hogshead, ordinarily used to store ale, for a home. He was, of course, a fisherman, as were many of the first Europeans in Marblehead. There was Thomas Graye, for instance, who both fished and traded on Cape Ann. Isaac Allerton and Moses Maverick or John Peach, for whom Peach's Point was named, all were fishermen.

On December 12, 1648, independence came to Marblehead. The Salem Town Meeting voted, subject to the approval of the Massachusetts General Court, to grant its complete independence from Salem. Governance was established through a Board of Selectmen. In 1684, the town received a deed from the tribe that gave the town 3,700 acres known as "Marblehead." The deed, given at a cost of sixteen pounds sterling, can be found today hanging in the Selectmen's room at Abbot Hall.

The ubiquitous English Captain John Smith had been there, too. He had called it "Marble Harbour," but that name didn't last either. The granite ledges that could be seen from the ocean appeared to be metamorphic rather than igneous rock, and the place became known as Marblehead.

The town had narrow streets that smelled of codfish that were dried at the waterfront. The crooked streets of the village were continued inland as time went on, though the fishing nature of the town did not change. In fact, it thrived. That was due to there being plenty of fish a short distance from the shore. This wealth of opportunity became known on the southern and eastern ports of England as well as the Channel Islands, and fishermen came to Marblehead to make a living. The King's Royal Agent, after visiting Marblehead in 1660, returned to England and declared that Marblehead was "…the Greatest Towne for Fishing in New England."

The fishing industry in Marblehead grew steadily, and, by the year 1837, the fleet of fishing vessels had reached almost a hundred. However, this heyday was near an end, scuttled by a single event. On September 19, 1846, the fleet was caught in a terrible storm while fishing for cod on the Grand Banks. The hurricane winds caught them off guard, destroying or damaging large numbers of ships. They lost sixty-five sailors, and that began the decline of the town's fishing industry. It still has those who make their livings by trawling the deep or taking lobsters, but Marblehead never regained the worldwide reputation for fishing that it once had.

Still, Marblehead did not abandon its use of the sea or love for things nautical. Rather than sailing vessels from which to fish, the town turned to

New York Fleet in MARBLEHEAD HARBOR, showing Old Town.

Protected by Ft. Sewall at its mouth, and with rocky outcrops, Marblehead Harbor was too dangerous for British ships to enter. *Postcard 1908.*

boats that sailed for pleasure and for the fun of competing in races. The sailing craft in the harbor are the equal of any small harbor in America, and it has served as the base for a number of international boat races, including those whose courses run to Spain, Germany, and Bermuda.

Perhaps best known is the biennial race, Marblehad-to-Halifax Ocean Race, that began in 1905, running to Halifax, Nova Scotia, which continues to be run every other year. It begins in the afternoon in Marblehead Harbor at the buoy "Tinker's Gong" and observers on board claim that as many as a thousand boats can be seen. The race is a challenge for even talented sailors, with the unpredictable weather and tricky tides in the Gulf of Maine and the Bay of Fundy making navigation difficult. Also, Marblehead Race Week is held each July, a tradition that goes back to 1889. The regatta brings yachtsmen from all over the world and helps the town hold the title of "Yachting Capital of the World."

It's not surprising that sailors from Marblehead played a significant part in the forming of our nation, when the colonies broke away from the British over issues of control and taxation. Colonel John Glover, who organized a militia in town, was given command of the 21st Regiment on the eve of the fortification and subsequent battle of Bunker Hill. General Washington chartered Glover's schooner, the aforementioned *Hannah*, as a privateer. It was outfitted at Beverly and set sail on September 5, 1775, making it the first American war ship.

The men from Marblehead became known as "Glover's Regiment," and after the fighting around Boston, they moved on to New York as the 14th Continental Regiment, an amphibious regiment who famously rescued the army by ferrying Washington's men across the East River to Manhattan after the defeat at the Battle of Long Island. They gained even more fame by rowing Washington's army across the ice-choked Delaware River late at night, as a prelude to his surprise attack on the Hessians and victory at Trenton, on Christmas 1776, as depicted in Emanuel Leutze's painting, *Washington Crossing the Delaware*.

Glover's ship *Hannah* was commanded by another seaman from Marblehead. Nicholas Broughton and four other Glover vessels served in similar roles, three of them with townsmen at the helm.

John Glover was a hero of the Battle of Long Island and rowed Washington and his men across the ice-clogged Delaware during the Revolution. His 1762 house still stands in Marblehead. *Sketch, 1900.*

Old Ironsides eluded British warships by entering Marblehead Harbor. In 1997, it sailed from Boston to Marblehead in commemoration. *Photo by U.S. Navy by Journalist 1st Class Matt Chabe.*

Marblehead's harbor also played a role in the War of 1812 when "Old Ironsides" (USS *Constitution*) used it as a haven as it was being followed by two British frigates. The American ship had several native Marbleheaders on board who knew the rocky shallows of the harbor and could guide the navigation. However, the British had no charts of the channels and could also view the cannon at Fort Sewall at the mouth of the harbor, which would have endangered them if they had tried to enter. So, they stood off and then retreated. This occasion was celebrated in 1997 when the USS *Constitution*, on its 200th birthday, sailed from its home in Charlestown to Marblehead Harbor, under its own power for the first time in 116 years. Fort Sewall played a role many years before the Revolution, when Henry Frankland went to Marblehead Harbor to inspect its fortifications.

William Starling Burgess built a yacht yard in Marblehead. In 1908, having become interested in aviation, he joined A.M. Herring and built the first biplane—*The Flying Fish*—at his Marblehead boatyard. Burgess joined his interests to launch Marblehead as the "Birthplace of Marine Aviation." It made a test flight over Marblehead Harbor in 1911, that is marked with a plaque in Hammond Park. Both the U.S. Navy and the Canadian Aviation Corps ordered the new flying boat. Burgess also designed three yachts that, at various times, have won the America's Cup races.

Marblehead has plenty of history, even without special events. It has preserved many of its historic centuries-old homes on its crooked lanes, and numerous historic sights, along with the still-active marine life of its harbor.

⚓

Swampscott

LAND OF THE RED ROCK

Shaped like a triangle, with the longest side along the ocean, the town of Swampscott covers barely three square miles. Not surprisingly, the geography has largely determined its history. Fishing, seafaring, and vacationing have been mainstays of the economy there.

Fishing was also a pursuit of the Naumkeag Indians, who dwelled there before the first Puritans arrived, and stayed for some time after that. Like other Indians along the coast, the Naumkeags were helpful to the colonists. The Naumkeags themselves called the area the "land of the red rock." The name of the town comes from two Indian words, *Ompsk* meaning "rock" and *Musqui*, meaning "red." So, it means "at the red rock," which is how the Naumkeag Indians described the place. They fished and hunted there when Francis Ingalls arrived at Humphrey's Brook, in 1629, and built the first tannery in the Massachusetts Bay Colony.

Swampscott began as a small fishing village and built a large fleet of commercial fishing boats. The early written accounts indicate that one out of three men who lived there was a fisherman. But shoemakers, farmers, and merchants also dwelled at the location. One of them was quite enterprising.

Ebeneezer Phillips kept his eyes and ears open, and, in the late 1700s, learned from the Naumkeags (who were still around at the time) a method

Along this stretch is the Swampscott Fish House, the oldest active fish house in the country. It is also home to the Swampscott Yacht Club and the Swampscott Sailing Program. *Postcard, 1910.*

of drying fish. He dried cod, put them in barrels and shipped them all over the world. The process of drying fish to preserve them was important because vessels that were fishing off the Grand Banks couldn't return frequently to Europe with the fish they had taken. Naturally, price depended on quality, and quality depended on freshness.

The process seems unremarkable, but Phillips managed to systematize and expand it, making Indian lore into a business so successful that he became America's first millionaire by salting the fish held in the boat. The result was known as a "fishbulk."

A boatload of salt would be rowed alongside the ship and a sail was let down to serve as a sort of funnel. Then, men with large, wooden shovels would throw the salt up onto the deck, while singing a sea shanty in an even-paced singsong manner that allowed all of them to time their shoveling so the salt cascaded down in unison. Sea shanties varied according to the task, but they served to synchronize movements and made the work less tedious.

The salt preserved and cured the fish and this process was used until the time when refrigeration was available. When the time came to remove the fish from the fishbulk, it was washed clean of the excess salt and taken to the "fish flakes" in wheelbarrows. These were platforms built on stilts along the shore, with boughs of evergreens across the top. They were used to dry fish—mostly cod—in the sun. The fish were laid out head to tail to make the best use of space. They were first placed face-up and then turned over so both sides were dried.

As the air became damp, either at night or on a rainy day, the fish were gathered into piles called "faggots," then stored in a warehouse or shed until all the season's harvest of fish was ready for shipping. The whole drying process may have taken a couple of months. The fish were stored in barrels when ready to be transported. We can only assume that Phillips set up a place that became recognized as the location for depositing fish for drying and shipping, and thus cornered the market early on.

That worked for Swampscott as did other inventions. Another Ebenezer, this one Ebenezer Thorndike, invented the lobster pot in 1808 to make harvesting lobsters much faster. Also, the Swampscott Dory was invented in 1840 by Theophilus Brackett. Used initially to row and pull lobster pots, it was such a seaworthy, flat-bottomed boat that it was used around the world—and still is in use. Another, larger vessel was the *Schooner of Swampscott*, a fore-and-aft rigged sailing vessel used primarily for the coastal trade.

In 1881, Charles Reed, a summer visitor and Civil War hero, designed the town seal, for which he was paid $12. It shows the deck of a small fishing schooner with Capt. James Phillips at the tiller, dressed in a sou'wester.

The town also boasts an old (1798) English cannon decorated with royal arms that was captured by the ship *Grand Turk* when serving as a privateer during the War of 1812. The cannon was bought by the Swampscott fishermen in 1835 for use as a fog signal. The last time it was used, on Independence Day in 1857, two men were killed as they tried to fire it. It now stands at Monument Square.

The *Grand Turk* was America's first great merchant ship and was used in the China trade. Its owner, millionaire Elias Hacket Derby, is known also for the rarity of having one blue and one brown eye.

Another part of Swampscott's history, also linked with the sea, was its era of large homes and resorts, built during the 19th century and used by wealthy people and businessmen from across the country. May of them returned and built great homes of their own, some of which gained historical significance. John Humphrey, who was the first deputy governor of Massachusetts Bay Colony, built a saltbox there in 1637, which is now the home of the historical society and is listed on the National Register of Historic Places. Also listed is the home of Elihu Thomson, whose electric company became General Electric. The Georgian house is now the town's administration building.

Another summer estate was that of Andrew Preston, who founded United Fruit. His summer home stood on 100 acres and included a golf course. Several of the first shingled homes in town were built by architect Arthur Little. All had ocean views and most came with ballrooms, too, in keeping with the fashion of the time.

Then there were the hotels and boarding houses that served summer visitors, including the Ocean House, Hotel Preston, Lincoln House, Hotel Bellevue, and the New Ocean House. President Coolidge stayed here as did Ethel Donahue, heir to the F.W. Woolworth fortune. Although the hotels are gone, the aura of a summer resort remains along Swampscott's Atlantic coast, just north of Boston.

⚓

Egg Rock

SEA SERPENTS AND A RESCUE DOG

Egg Rock is a three-acre, whale-shaped island, about half a mile off the shore of Nahant, that rises about eighty feet above the water. A lighthouse was built there in order to protect the fishing boats that were leaving and entering Swampscott, particularly Fisherman's Beach. The numbers of men fishing from schooners off Swampscott had risen to well over 200 by the middle of the 19th century, and they were now deep sea fishing, as well.

Egg Rock was named for the nesting habits of sea gulls, who laid their eggs on the rocky island that lay in the path of these vessels. Owned originally by Salem, it was ceded in 1856 to the U.S. Government, after a number of Boston-based insurance companies petitioned Congress to erect a lighthouse on this dangerous site.

As a result, a two-story house for the keeper was built with a fixed white light on its roof in a tower. The light was changed to fixed red after a shipwreck in which the captain mistook the light for Long Island, south of Boston. The tower was raised in 1870 to 198 feet.

A similar story can be told for many islands and lighthouses on the Atlantic Coast, but Egg Rock has some interesting sub-stories. One has to do with a dog named Milo, kept by the lighthouse keeper (as many lonely lighthouses and their keepers keep dogs). Milo, however, had special talents and interests. He was a large dog, a mixture of St. Bernard and Newfoundland, and owned by George Taylor, the first keeper of the light on Egg Rock. On foggy nights, Milo would bark to warn approaching ships of the looming rocks.

Milo was also something of a retriever. One time, the keeper was shooting at sea birds and hit a loon. The bird fell into the sea, a fair distance off shore, but was not fatally wounded. Milo swam out after the bird to bring it back, but just as he got near, the bird was able to fly off for a short distance. Milo did not give up, but pursued the bird. The same thing occurred over and over, until Milo disappeared over the horizon.

Some paintings deliver the narrative, as this one, showing Milo, the amazing dog who rescued many small children off Egg Rock lighthouse near Nahant. Sir Edwin Henry Landseer painted this scene, using the lighthouse keeper's son as a model. *Edwin Landseer, oil on canvas, 1856.*

He did not re-appear during the rest of the day. But the following day, Milo came swimming over from Nahant, where it seems he had spent the night, recovering his strength after his long swim.

With his new reputation for swimming, fishermen on the island had sport with Milo by binding bundles of sticks with codfish and tossing the bundle out into the tides. Milo would unfailingly retrieve the bundles and enjoy rewards. But he also saved swimmers from drowning. The lifesaving dog became famous when the well-known English painter, Sir Edwin Henry Landseer, painted a picture of Milo with the keeper's son, Fred, between his paws, in a beachside survival scene entitled "Saved."

The painting became quite popular in the mid-19th century. Landseer was something of a curiosity himself, inasmuch as he could paint with both hands at the same time. For example, he could paint a dog's head and snout with his left hand while the right hand was painting the dog's tail.

In 1897, fire destroyed the Egg Rock lighthouse and it was replaced by a thirty-two-foot-high white, square brick tower. Shortly thereafter, another keeper, George Lyon, built a landing stage on the island with a hoist that would lift a boat out of the water onto the deck of the boathouse.

The fishing industry in that area declined, until only a few dozen fishermen remained by World War I. The light was left dark during the war years, lest an enemy submarine use it as a homing beacon.

After the war, an automated light was installed. In 1922, the light was decommissioned. The government sold the lighthouse for $160 with the understanding that whoever bought it must remove the lighthouse. A crew removed the building from its foundation, put it on rollers, and moved it downhill in order to load it onto a barge. However, a rope snapped and the house plunged into the ocean.

Egg Rock is today, fittingly, a bird sanctuary called the Henry Cabot Lodge Wildlife Sanctuary, for the U.S. senator who did much to preserve the habitat. You can see Egg Rock as you walk or drive along Lynn Shore Drive.

But the story is deeper than the waters around Egg Rock. The area is also famous for the legend of an immense sea serpent that has been seen over hundreds of years, from the time of the local Indian tribes right up through the 20th century.

An early colonial, Obadiah Turner, described it as "… a wonderful big serpent lying on ye water, and reaching from Nahantus to ye great rocke wich we call Birdds Egg Rodke." Observers rushed to the coast just before the Civil War, according to noted writer Henry David Thoreau, who wrote in his journal, in 1858, that hundreds of people in Swampscott had seen the serpent and that: "The road from Boston was lined with people directly, coming to see the monster …" There was an intensive period of sightings in August 1817, when the serpent visited Gloucester Harbor and nearby areas every day for a month.

It was typically described as sixty feet or more in length, brown in color, moving in an up and down undulation (not sideways like a snake), and with a large head shaped like a horse's. The New England Linnaean Society in Boston set out to collect evidence to try to get a scientific hold on this phenomenon. They took depositions from people who claimed to have seen it. Their observations varied in details, but were surprisingly similar. All agreed it was like nothing else they'd ever seen.

The "Merchant Prince" of Boston, Thomas Handasyd Perkins, no stranger to marine phenomena, saw the creature through a spyglass and described it, as others had, but noted a "long marline-spike [*sic*] horn on its head." The creature would appear nearly every summer thereafter for a century.

People who reported sightings were, of course, ridiculed, including a judge from New York. Perhaps the strangest report came from a fishing vessel that was attacked in a *Jaws*-like way by the creature that came up from beneath a net full of mackerel, moved alongside the boat, and was caught up in the net. The crew claimed to have cut it to pieces and released it from the net rather than towing it in. All of the fish they had caught escaped and the crew was exhausted from the fight, but the captain later regretted not bringing in the proof.

Proof seems to have been hard to come by, and so have sightings in recent years, there having been few in the past half century. A sighting was made in 1960 by a charter boat with seven on board in Gloucester Harbor, but that was a rarity in modern times. Some speculate that the advent of engines in boats and ships alerts the creature to their presence, and it stays away.

⚓

Nahant

ALMOST AN ISLAND

The peninsula we know as Nahant was bought and paid for by a new suit of clothes. Thomas "Farmer" Dexter paid that much for it in 1632 in trade with the Indian sachem who owned it, a man called "Black Will," because of his dark complexion. Dexter lived not far away on the Saugus River, near the ironworks. He bought the land for speculation, but apparently Black Will sold the same land to several people, and that resulted in lawsuits years later. The area was used to grow wheat and graze animals in the early days, but otherwise remained uninhabited for many years, although Dexter built a fence across the causeway to keep out wolves. A court took away his disputed title to the land.

The Indians named it *Nahant*, or "almost an island," although their original name *Nahanten* refers to twin things, in this case the two islands that make up the present rocky peninsula at the end of a causeway built upon barrier beach and sand dunes.

Nahant was first settled in 1630 as part of Lynn. Isaac Johnson's servants brought his cattle to Lynn where they grazed, and others did the same with their cattle, sheep, and goats. Up until the turn of the 19th century, only three homes stood on the island, including that of the Johnsons, built by Jeremy Gray.

It was the Johnsons who built the first hotel in 1802, but others would follow in times to come. Other improvements included a steamboat to Boston each day, beginning in 1817. Six years later, Nahant Road was laid out and a stagecoach used it.

When the temperance movement clamped a ban on the use of alcohol in 1853, Nahant separated from Lynn and incorporated on its own in order to protect its summer tourist trade, which, for many years, was Nahant's main industry. Late in the 1800s, Nahant was home to some of the country's early amusement parks, hotels, and many homes for people who summered there. In the 20th century, that trolleys ran here from Lynn. In 1832, the first church was erected, always a marker that indicates the permanence of a community.

⚓

The Pirates of Dungeon Rock

A North Shore mystery stems from the 17th century, in Lynn Harbor, at the Saugus River, about one mile from Nahant. A black ship, bearing no flag of any nation, appeared without notice in the harbor at Lynn in the last days of summer in the year 1658. In those days of few settlers and much danger, colonists frequently looked to the sea, which would have provided a likely source of threat from non-English ships and might carry hostile crews. So it's not surprising that the ship drew attention almost at once.

The citizens who spotted the ship were alarmed by it. They quickly spread the word that pirates had moored in the harbor. Nor did the ship settle at anchor or sail away. Those on board lowered a boat into the harbor and loaded a chest into it. Then four men began to row the boat up the Saugus River, landing near theSaugus Iron Works. All this was done quickly and silently, viewed only from afar. The ship that had been anchored off shore then disappeared.

The next day, as workmen showed up to begin their labor at the foundry, they noticed a note affixed to the door. It could only have been left by the pirates who had landed their boat at the site.

The note suggested a trade. The pirates, though they didn't identify themselves as such, needed certain items that could be provided by the workers who were skilled at making such things, or could certainly obtain them. They wanted tools, such as shovels, hatchets, and shackles, and would give silver in exchange for them. A place was designated where the tools could be left, with the promise that they would be replaced by silver coins.

This all came to pass; the tools were made and delivered and silver was left to pay for them. Mysteriously, even though some of the workers stood watch, no boat or ship had been sighted. The men and their vessel were gone.

Months later, the men reappeared, finding a very secluded spot for their hideout. It was in a deep valley, with high rocks and hills on two sides, as well as tall trees that shut out the sun for all but a few hours of the day. From the top of the rocks, the view on all sides was expansive, including the bay to the south. It has since been called Pirate's Glen. There they could see without being seen. They built a hut, started a garden and dug a well (whose remains are still there). People believe they buried treasure there as well, but searches have found nothing.

After a time, reports of the pirates reached authorities and a British ship was sent to hunt for them. Three pirates were captured and taken to England to be hung, but the fourth, Thomas Veal, escaped, heading deep into the Lynn Woods. Legend has it that Veal found a natural cave and made it his home, eventually becoming a cobbler and living in peace with the Lynn community.

An earthquake (but not the Cape Ann quake) struck the area and broke off a huge piece of rock that sealed the opening of Veal's cave. Veal, with all his possessions, was crushed or trapped and sealed forever within the cave henceforth called "Dungeon Rock," or alternatively "Pirate's Rock." It is located atop high hills that command a view of 50 miles north and south, including the nearby Saugus River and the harbor. It would have provided good cover for pirates to see ships dock and for them to steal furtively down the stream for an attack (though we have no record that this ever happened and would be unlikely for Veal to have attempted by himself.

The remains of Thomas Veal and his treasure were left undisturbed for nearly 200 years. In the 1830s, two attempts were made to recover the treasure by placing kegs of powder at the cave opening and igniting them. Both attempts failed, and the opening to the cave was destroyed, but no riches were found.

Twenty-two years after this, Hiram Marble, a member of the Spiritualist Church from Charlton, Massachusetts, came to Pirate's Rock. Like other spiritualists, Marble believed it was possible to talk to people in the afterlife. He thought he had, received a message from Thomas Veal from beyond the grave. Veal's ghost told him to come to Pirate's Rock and dig. If he did, he would get rich.

Marble and his family also realized that if they pulled this off, it would boost the reputation of Spiritualism and also make them wealthy. So Hiram bought five acres around the cave and began digging. In their time at Pirate's Rock, the Marbles built and lived in a wooden house two floors high, and built other structures as well. Remnants of the foundation can still be found, as can remnants of other buildings.

Once Hiram completed his living quarters, his wife and son Edwin joined him. After a time, his son helped him with his digging. It was a slow, difficult process. They would dig and try to blast the solid rock at a discouragingly slow pace—perhaps only a foot a month. This called for drilling a line of holes into the rock and filling them with black powder, setting a fuse, lighting it and then running to a safe distance.

The debris they loosened or displaced was carted out of the tunnel and left on the hillside. This disposed material formed a gravelly area outside the tunnel, which provided evidence of their doings to those who explored the area later and tried to piece things together.

Not only was the digging process long and tedious, but it was expensive, and, in time, Hiram and Edwin began to run thin on funds. They decided to offer tours to the curious, for which they charged a quarter. They also sold bonds on the future bonanza that they hoped for. The cost of these was a dollar. These, of course, were in Civil War-era currency, when a dollar bought lots more.

The Marbles realized that success would come more quickly if they had a better idea of where to dig. As Spiritualists, they naturally turned to people they knew. These people were mediums, who claimed the ability to communicate with the dead. During séances, Hiram would write questions and wad the paper so it couldn't be read. The medium would then write an answer to the hidden questions without reading the question.

A tour of the tunnel, would reveal abrupt changes in direction. The spirits would lead the diggers in one direction and then another, creating a twisting path into the rock. The spirits reassured the Marbles by telling them that, like Moses, wandering the desert for forty years, it was necessary for them to toil before they received their reward.

Hiram passed away in 1868 without ever finding his treasure. His son, Edwin, dug on until his death in 1880. Edwin's last wish was to be buried at Dungeon Rock. At the top of a set of stairs beginning next to the old cellar hole, you will find a large pink piece of rock. This stone marks the grave of Edwin Marble and the end of the quest for treasure.

It is interesting to note that the Marbles did not seek the treasure for themselves. They labored to achieve two goals. The first was to prove that they could communicate with people in the afterlife. At this they failed. The second goal was achieved, but not in the way the Marbles envisioned. Living in this beautiful setting for so many years gave the Marbles a vision of a free public forest, a park for all to enjoy. In that, they succeeded. Hiram planned to take his pirate treasure and purchase as much land as possible for the people of Lynn to enjoy forever. The citizens of Lynn purchased the land shortly after Edwin's death, to form the new park, Lynn Woods.

⚓

Lynn

LEATHER, ELECTRICITY, AND ENGINES

"Why thus alone are you ploughing, Mr. Thrifty?"
"O sir, my boys have all left me and turned shoepeggers."
Farmer's Almanac, 1834

Several towns in Massachusetts became known for their shoemaking industries, and the North Shore town of Lynn was the leader among them.

In earlier colonial times, most settlers made shoes for themselves and their families, learning the craft from those who had brought their skills with them from England. This was New England, however. They had to raise food and perhaps sell or trade some of the produce for other things they needed. But New England also came with four seasons, and that meant that a good part of the year was too cold and the ground was too hard to plant and raise crops.

After a time, some who were farmers became shoemakers during the winter, going from house to house or setting up workshops on their own land. These shops were called "ten-footers" for their size, and the men of the family made the leather and soles, while inside the house, women and girls worked on sewing the uppers. A few men were itinerants who went from family to family, staying a week or so and making shoes in their kitchen for everyone in the family—all the while perhaps passing on the news or gossip they had gathered in their travels.

By the early 1800s, a few factories were established, where craftsmen brought their work to be assembled. Toward the middle of the 19th century, workers reported to factories where all operations were performed under one roof. Towns like Lynn, Weymouth, and Brockton became leaders with many factories and workers producing quality output that was sold outside of town and even outside the country.

Various factors led to these towns becoming shoemaking centers instead iron foundries, woolen plants, paper mills, furniture factories, and agricultural centers.

Shoe factories needed working capital, so it helped if they were near Boston, where the banks and investors were located. They needed to ship their finished products, so they needed to be near the coast, and they had to be near large tanneries to get various qualities of leather. Some towns met those needs and had ready labor, so factories began there. As the number of factories grew, certain towns developed a tradition for shoemaking and that led to more factories.

Lynn was such a place. It was located on the coast, near Boston, used the regional tannery in Peabody, and began by producing the boots worn by George Washington's soldiers during the Revolutionary War. So, it had a running start in becoming a shoemaking town.

After the Revolution, it was shoemaking that drove the growth of the town well into the 19th century. Lynn led the way in turning out shoes and boots, and was particularly a leader in the production of women's and children's shoes.

As an early seaport, Lynn merchants had imported fancy shoes from abroad, mostly from England. Though they sold those imports, they also copied them, and Lynn factories competed among themselves to make the best and latest versions of shoes of all types.

Until the middle of the 1800s, skilled craftsmen made shoes by hand. Then a number of American inventors developed machines to perform the tasks specific to shoemaking. When Elias Howe invented the sewing machine, in 1841, it was adapted for use in stitching the upper parts of shoes together. Not long afterwards, Lyman Blake made a variation on Howe's machine that sewed soles to uppers. The Abington-born inventor, Blake worked for Isaac Singer's sewing machine company, going from factory to factory and setting up machines, and later worked for Gordon McKay. In 1858, Blake patented a machine that he sold to his boss, who named it the McKay machine.

In the second half of the 19th century, after the Industrial Revolution, most shoemaking operations had been mechanized to some extent. Machines had been invented that would cut, sew, and tack shoes, but the one operation that seemed to defy the march of machines was "lasting"—attaching the uppers to the soles. Good lasting added to the quality of a shoe, allowing it to fit well, look good and be comfortable for walking. A "last" was a model of the foot made out of wood, and it took a special skill to stretch the leather over the last and then to tack the finished shape in place.

The fastest way to "last" was by pegging and stitching, using wooden pegs about ¾" in length. Lasting was a skill known to a limited number of people, and it took longer than the other operations. In fact, "lasters" had banded together and some thought that they intentionally slowed things down as a work action to gain larger wages. Most people thought that it would be impossible to make a machine that would do this work, so these men had lasting power.

A machine that would do that work would have been as important as Elias Howe's sewing machine or Eli Whitney's cotton gin—at least to the shoe industry. Most people thought it couldn't be done and that "lasting" would always be done by hand. It would take, in fact, an extraordinary person to come up with that invention. Such a person was on his way to Lynn by the 1870s.

Inventing a Faster Laster

His name was Jan Matzeliger and he came to America from what is now the country of Surinam on the northern coast of South America. Jan was born to a black native woman, who was a slave, and a Dutch engineer. At age 10, he worked in his father's machine shop as an apprentice and visited factories where he showed an unusual skill for repairing machines. Like such men at any time, those who can fix things were in demand, and Jan was more than just a good mechanic. Jan was fascinated by machines. They became almost an obsession with him.

When he was 19, he went to sea on an East Indian merchant ship. For two years he sailed to the Far East and also repaired the ship's engines. When the ship docked in Philadelphia, he stayed there. He quickly learned English, finding employment in a shoemaking factory where he learned to use a MacKay machine.

People who saw his interest in learning shoemaking suggested that he go to Lynn, where more than half the shoes in America were made at the time. (Ironically, the seaport of Gloucester, Massachusetts, regularly sent ships to Surinam. Had Jan known it, he would have wound up in Lynn sooner had he boarded one of those ships.)

As a black man with only a crude use of English, he had trouble finding a job, but finally became an apprentice in the Harney shoe factory. He operated the well-known MacKay machine to stitch the soles of a shoe. As Jan Matzeliger learned the trade, he came to recognize that the slow and most costly part of the operation was "lasting." He knew that people didn't think a machine could do this work, but Matzeliger felt they were wrong. He could make such a machine.

Jan was a "bootstraps" kind of guy. After a full day of work, he went to night school, improved his English, and began to read books on physics and mechanics. He saved his money to buy his own books. Matzeliger also had talent as an artist. He painted pictures and gave them to his friends, and also taught courses in oil painting to earn a little extra money. After working a while, he earned enough to buy a set of drawing instruments and began to put his ideas onto paper.

But he wanted to learn more, so he applied for the job of millwright in his factory. This put him in charge of maintaining and repairing machines, and it allowed him to go everywhere in the factory and observe—always observe. He especially observed the "lasters" at work, and he began to understand how they worked and how he could imitate their movements with a machine.

Matzeligere began to draw plans for a new piece of equipment that would do the work of the lasters. But he did it secretly. He rented an unheated room in the West Lynn Mission, where he worked on his plans for a lasting machine. After six months (using cigar boxes, wire, nails and scraps of wood), he made a model of his machine. Crude as it was, a professional inventor offered him $50 for the plan, but he declined. Next, he tried to make a machine from scraps of iron. This lasting machine took four years of labor and drew an offer of $1,500, which he also turned down.

He continued to work on perfecting his machine in a corner of the factory floor where he worked. He slept little and spent only a small amount on food, so he could use the money for his project. It was lonely work, taking ten years, and it gained him mostly ridicule.

Jan had learned that he would need a patent for his invention, and funds to go through the patent process, so he looked for help. Making an agreement with Charles H. Delnow and Melville S. Nichols, they would provide financial backing, and he agreed to give them each a third of the ownership rights in return. When he submitted his drawings of the machine to the U.S. Patent Office, the people there could not understand them, because they were too complex. Instead, someone had to be sent to Lynn to see him run the machine, and decide whether it worked the way it was supposed to.

His machine held the wooden last in place, pulled the leather over it, fitted it at the heel and at the toe, then moved the last forward, and drove in the nails, all in one minute. On March 20, 1883, Matzeliger, Delnow, and Nichols received the patent.

Next, came a public demonstration. In May 1885, the machine was first tested in a factory; it passed with flying colors, breaking a record for a lasting operation by doing seventy-five pairs of shoes. As he improved his machine, it was able to produce 700 pairs of shoes in a day.

Now it was ready to be mass-produced. Two others joined Jan and his partners to raise the required funds. The new partnership was called the Consolidated Lasting Machine Company. Matzeliger sold his rights for stock in the company, which would become the United Shoe Machinery Company (later, in Beverly).

Matzeliger, however, didn't get to enjoy the fruits of his labor. He died of tuberculosis in 1889 at age 37. His hard work and creativity enabled shoe factories to produce for less, pay better wages to more workers, and sell their shoes in quantity at lower prices. As often happens, it wasn't the inventor who profited the most. Matzeliger's patents were bought and eventually came under control of the new United Shoe Machinery Company capitalized at $20 million. The company's business was so successful that the price of shoes was cut in half everywhere across the country. And in a win-win situation, they were able to double the wages of the workers and improve the working conditions for millions of shoemaking workers.

United Shoe didn't sell their machines, though. They leased them; like some of today's software companies, those who leased the machines were given the chance to upgrade them with new parts when improved machines came along. Buying the upgrade didn't mean you owned the machine, though. You only got the new parts. Leasers were also charged according to the number of times they used the machines (which came with a counter to tabulate usage). The United Shoe Machinery Company got what amounted to a "royalty" on each pair of shoes made with their machines. They were, of course, a monopoly and had to fight many lawsuits because of it.

As a side note: In addition to "the Shoe" in Beverly, United Shoe also built the first skyscraper in Boston (which still stands as part of the Landmark Building).

In time, increased speed of production depressed wages, and after an economic depression, companies rehired their laid-off workers at lower rates. A union was formed and that was followed, in 1860, by a massive strike of 20,000 workers in Lynn and surrounding towns. The strike and the protest march that followed gained national attention. Even Abraham Lincoln commented. He told a reporter that he was:

> glad to see that a system of labor prevails in New England under which laborers can strike when they want to, where they are not obliged to labor whether you pay them or not. I like a system which lets a man quit when he wants to, and wish it might prevail everywhere.

Lincoln's words didn't sway the factory owners, though. The strike failed, and the Civil War that followed muted the demands of laborers. By the end of the Civil War, 27,000 people lived in Lynn and it had 200 shoe-related businesses. Towards the end of the 19th century, other industries began to make an impact in Lynn.

The electric industry became another mainstay and, surprisingly, an offshoot from shoemaking. Charles Coffin, with other shoe company investors, formed a partnership with businessman Abbott Barton, in 1883, in an incipient move that would lead to the formation of a great international company. Coffin was a brilliant businessman who had earned a fortune in shoemaking. He teamed with Barton to buy a faltering electric business from New Britain, Connecticut, and moved it to Western Avenue in Lynn. The "plum" of the business from Connecticut was, not a piece of machinery or a manufacturing process—it was a person. Elihu Thomson was a prolific, British-born, medal-winning inventor. (Thomson was ahead of everyone in recognizing the dangers of x-rays.) The new electric company was called Houston-Thomson International. Like many innovators and others who have improved the human condition, Thomson is largely forgotten today, but the effects of his contributions live on.

At around the same time, Thomas Edison had combined his several titles under the name of Edison General Electric, in Schenectady, New York. The two companies merged in 1892 as "General Electric" with plants in both cities.

Motors, meters, and electric lights were produced in Lynn to begin with, but the plant later produced aircraft electrical systems and engines, especially during the Second World War. After that, in conjunction with Massachusetts Institute of Technology (M.I.T.), the Lynn plant made jet engines. In 2010, GE was ranked the second largest company in the world by *Forbes* magazine.

The Great Lynn Depot War

Lynn, Lynn, city of sin
You never come out the way you went in.
Ask for water, they give you a gin;
the girls say no, but always give in.

At the end of the Civil War, in 1865, Lynn, Massachusetts, was a place poised for growth. A big part of the growth would depend on railroads that would bring freight to and from Lynn's factories, as well as people to work and live there.

The Eastern Railroad played an important role in the development of the North Shore. It was big, it was pioneering, but it was not a monopoly; and railroads that have to compete have to be awfully good and gratefully lucky.

Eastern ran from Boston to Portland, Maine, competing with the Boston and Maine Railroad (B&M). Eastern had an advantage over the B&M because its tracks hugged the shore, whereas those of B&M ran farther inland. Eastern was able to serve large coastal locations at Lynn, Salem, Beverly, and Newburyport, with their many industries and a large population of potential passengers.

Eastern also had a disadvantage. It had made poor choices in the placement of its terminals, especially in Boston where the tracks stopped in East Boston, so patrons had to take a short ferry ride into the city. Is that any way to run a railroad? Here was an obvious weakness that a competitor could one day exploit. It ought to have been fixed. But that wasn't the only problem.

Eastern's first thrust into Lynn was also problematic. The Eastern depot in Lynn was located at Central Square. However, that was not the commercial center of town. Market Street was where the merchants wanted a new depot. It was *time* for a new depot, and Eastern seemed to have a chance to correct its initial error, but Central Square advocates would not yield easily. So a conflict developed. It would be known as "The Great Lynn Depot War." Having a fancy new depot became a matter of civic pride.

Eastern began to feel pressure for a Market Street depot, but the State Legislature interfered. The folks at the capitol on Beacon Hill decided that they ought to be the ones to make important decisions, like where to put a train terminal, so they passed a law that any depot that had been in place for five years or more could not be abandoned without the consent of the legislature.

Eastern was charged with political chicanery, and the dispute finally wound up in the U.S. Supreme Court. They ruled that two depots must be built.

In 1873, just months after a second depot had been built on Market Street, Eastern got legislative permission to demolish it. None of this did Eastern any good. The building of two depots plus the legal bills cost Eastern $300,000 and a lot of bad public relations. Government intervention proved to be a failure.

Known popularly as the "Narrow Gauge" for the width of its tracks, the new road ran right along Revere Beach and brought many new people to the area. *Mason Bogie steam locomotive. Builder's photograph taken 1886.*

One company's disaster was another company's opportunity. Around this time, Albert P. Blake began to get support for an alternative railroad that would run along the shore from Boston to Lynn, with a depot on Market Street. Albert's brain was sharply honed. People would later learn that he had more than transportation in mind. His real thrust would be in real estate. Like Henry Whitney in Brookline, Blake proposed to provide transportation to new areas and to sell lots and housing along the route. Albert Blake realized that Boston was overcrowded. He thought it would be a good time for groups of financiers to pool their resources to develop real estate outside of the city and provide living space for people. His first venture was in Hyde Park, and it involved buying a railroad, as well as its trestle across the Neponset River, which would take the new residents to Boston and back. Next, Blake gazed thoughtfully on the area to the north of the city. He and his associates bought land north of Boston along the shore to Lynn. Much of this was marshland or salty soil, and he picked it up at fifty cents an acre—dirt-cheap.

The Boston, Revere Beach, and Lynn Railroad (popularly called the Narrow Gauge Railroad) did bring business and it did bring people, thanks in part to a smart advertising campaign, which caused the reader to imagine what it would be like to live in these new areas.

According to ad copy, the railroad offered:

> cheap, speedy, and direct transit to the seacoast and suburbs, and a chance for the middle class to buy pleasant homes near the city cheaply.

Albert and his associates learned what successful admen have come to know: if you talk to your audience about them and their needs, you'll get their attention. People attended, people bought, and then they moved to those new house lots in suburbia where Albert's railroad could take them. He built it; they came.

The railroad's effect was widespread. It also brought many visitors to Revere Beach, with words like these:

> The road will also be a godsend to the sweltering thousands of working men, women, and children of the city who might thus get a sniff of sea air and catch a glimpse of green fields and woods….

And, in fact, many of these sweltering thousands did want to "sniff" the ocean air and cool themselves in the surf. The railroad, which ran right along the crest of the beach, gave the view and the sniff without even leaving the train. But many did get off, and thousands settled in Revere and other towns along the water, thanks to the opening brought by the Narrow Gauge's thin thrust into this virgin territory. Some Revere residents, however, also "sniffed" when they thought of those sweltering thousands coming to a neighborhood near them. Thus, when the tracks from Lynn were to be joined with those of Revere, a huge crowd of protestors from Revere blocked the tracks and stopped the work. The train workers were sent home. The protestors said they were against the opportunists who would be using the railroad to exploit the area, but that wasn't all that was bothering some of them: "We don't want all the riffraff from Boston at our back doors," was one quote. The railroad, however, did an end-around. While the town slept, the workers returned and completed the track.

The new road was officially called the Boston, Revere Beach, and Lynn Railroad, but because of the size of its track, it was commonly called the Narrow Gauge Railroad. It was less than nine miles in length, and its track was approximately three feet apart. The new line opened on July 29, 1875 and lasted until 1940, running from the Ferry Terminal in East Boston, where the Boston & Albany RR's boats docked, north along the coast through East Boston, Winthrop, and Revere, to the new terminal in Lynn. It included a three-mile-roll along the beach, with ocean breezes and the rumble of surf. The railroad would last but sixty-five years, and its effects remain today.

⚓

Revere

THE PEOPLE'S BEACH

The beach that became publicized by the Narrow Gauge Railroad became the first public beach in America. Just five miles north of Boston, it was called Revere Beach, but was also known as Crescent Beach, the people's beach, the Coney Island of New England, or the Atlantic City of New England. Revere Beach had, from its earliest days, easy access via transportation that made it accessible to the landlocked, and especially to city-dwellers.

As we've seen, a small railroad had a lot to do with popularizing the area and the beach, and making it accessible to the lower classes, but the Narrow Gauge also caused problems for those with a wider vision. In fact, the railroad almost made the beach a no-go. The heroic efforts of one of Boston's greatest landscape architects, Charles Eliot saved the beach for posterity. Like Teddy Roosevelt's efforts to establish the national parks, like Frederick Olmsted and the Emerald Necklace in Boston, Olmsted's disciple, Eliot, saved Revere and many other parkland and recreational areas in and around Boston.

The poorly capitalized Narrow Gauge didn't have the financial clout of its larger competitor, the Eastern Railroad. But it had a plan—in fact, a vision. That vision was a bit cloudy. The railroad was meant to serve the land on both sides of its eight-plus miles of track. Men who owned real estate in Winthrop, East Boston, and Revere and wanted to develop those sparsely-settled communities, started the railroad to accomplish that goal. And the railroad did add population to those places. Once it had done this "building up," it served the newer but still useful function of providing commuter service for people in those communities who worked in Boston.

But the Narrow Gauge will always be, and should be, remembered best for bringing prominence to Revere Beach. That was its key role in local history.

It was in 1875 that the Boston, Revere Beach, & Lynn Railroad built its line and allowed city people to travel to the beach. That much was fine, but the railroad also led to the development of hotels and other buildings right on the sand. Shoddy shacks hid the shoreline and larger buildings did the same.

Incredibly, the track of the railroad itself ran right along the crest of the beach. In fact, the BRB&L used this feature as a means of attracting passengers to the natural, beautiful views. They could sit by the windows and enjoy the sweep of ocean and beach as they rode to their destination. There were no roads or sidewalks along the beach, but bathers on the beach had to keep their eyes peeled for horses, wagons, and bicycles lest they get run over.

The railroad brought Revere's population from a sleepy 1,600-person town surrounded by marshland and water to a sizable town of nearly 5,000 just fifteen years after the last spike was driven to fasten down its narrow track. The trains seemed to have accomplished what their owners had wanted. The trouble was, it was hard to turn off the spigot once development started to pour. That beautiful crescent beach was on its way to becoming overrun and ruined, with buildings on the beach and severe over-development.

Each cloud has a bright ray, however. Because the railroad ran the length of the beach and separated it from the rest of the town, the land along the beach could not easily be subdivided. The development was spotty and disjointed, so when it came time to undo the harm, government agencies could deal with individuals who owned small pieces of land, rather than one or two powerful firms bristling with legal help.

Charles Eliot later commented on that when he walked onto the stage of Boston and North Shore history. A largely unknown landscape architect, Eliot was the prime mover in making the beach the wonder it was to become. By the middle 1890s, the state had created a Metropolitan Park Commission, whose purpose was to preserve certain natural areas in the Greater Boston region for recreation and the use for future generations.

Though not formally educated, Charles Eliot, the son of Harvard University President Charles William Eliot, decided he wanted to become a landscape architect like the great Frederick Law Olmsted who had created Central Park in New York and the Boston parkland system. Charles volunteered to work as an intern at Olmsted's firm and learned much from the master, by working on such projects as Franklin Park and the Arnold Arboretum.

In 1896, the state legislature authorized the Metropolitan Park Commission to take land at what became the Revere Beach Reservation. It was Eliot who would design this reservation. They cleared the beach of buildings, auctioning off some and having them moved, and destroying the rest. All of this (amazingly) was done within thirty days.

As for the Narrow Gauge Railroad that had inspired the growth but taken away the clean line of the beach, well, it was simply moved inland to the west, where today the public transit T line runs. A boulevard was built where the railroad had been. The Revere Beach, as we know it, was created.

Charles Eliot wanted free public access to the beach and fought many battles to preserve its curved vista. He insisted that all buildings that he had designed be placed to the west of the boulevard, and that these buildings must not spoil the view of the sweep of the shoreline.

Having demolished, flattened, and shaped, Eliot began to build. About halfway along the boulevard, he designed a brick bathhouse in Italian Renaissance style. It was divided into men's and women's sections with changing rooms off courtyards where swimwear was rented and donned. Tunnels were dug beneath the boulevard to allow swimmers to pass easily to the beach without having to cross the boulevard.

Along the beach side, three pairs of shaded pavilions were built, each with seating. Between the pair that lay opposite the bathhouse, a clock was erected with two faces. One side faced the ocean so that swimmers would not be late in returning the bathing suits they had rented for two hours. The other side allowed beachgoers to figure the times of tides and the nearness of the dinner hour.

At the south end of the beach, near Shirley Avenue, the layout was different. Here, a pair of pavilions was separated by a bandstand that saw frequent use in a day where outdoor concerts and musical bands were popular.

The final pair of pavilions stood at the northern end of the beach near Oak

Island. Next to the bathhouse was a police station built in a similar Italianate style. Its expanse included a house for the police commissioner, since his job also encompassed running the Revere Beach Reservation.

The beach had its grand opening on July 12, 1896, with about 45,000 people in attendance on that day, but it was only the beginning. The beach would show continued growth and development right up through World War II with some days during the 1920s and 1930s where the crowds reached 200,000 or more, the majority of them working-class people.

From *The Future in America*, the great British science-fiction writer H.G. Wells is quoted as saying:

> I suppose no city in all the world has ever produced so complete and ample a forecast of its own future as the Metropolitan Park Commission's plan for Boston.

Within five miles, inner city Bostonians had a world-class beach with inexpensive entertainment. It was a great place to bring the family, go on a date, or just enjoy the ambience—and there was plenty of that.

The beach would have the Great Ocean Pier, a 1,700-foot dance pavilion that was covered by a roof for all but 200 feet of its length. It also had ballrooms, such as the famous Oceanview and Beachview. Great American dance bands, including Jimmy and Tommy Dorsey, Paul Whiteman, Guy Lombardo, and Louis Prima played there.

Then, apart from the beach, but not by much, there was Wonderland. From 1906 until 1911, it was the world's first self-contained amusement park, twenty-six acres with all kinds of the latest amusements and rides. It also had special days with parades led by Alice in Wonderland. Admission was ten cents. Some believe it was the inspiration for Disneyland, which came years later. But alas, this expensive undertaking brought financial ruin to its owners and it closed within five years, though the spot did not remain bereft of entertainment. Another type appeared in 1935 when the Wonderland dog track was built on the same site and brought crowds looking for another type of recreation.

Wonderland lay slightly inland and was mostly a sideshow. Instead, the coastal boulevard would become the major locale for amusements, rides, bowling alleys, roller rinks, restaurants, hot dog stands and, later, pizza emporia, to say nothing of frozen custard treats at Mary Ahearn's and elsewhere. If readers of a certain age retain nostalgia for Revere Beach, it's likely they remember these things best.

In fact, most who recall Revere Beach will remark on the rides. At one time or another, there were four roller coasters. One was the "Lightning." It was all hills and drops. In fact, it was such an up-and-down ride that the only time you were on a level stretch was when you got on or off at the station. The Lightning was not on a par with modern coasters or even the "woodies" that remain from times past. It was far less safe. On the day it opened, a woman was killed and it closed down—for a scant twenty minutes. The next day, there were several injuries. So, you took your chances.

Far more dangerous-looking, but in fact safer because of its sounder engineering was the "Cyclone." This roller coaster became quite famous, and was the longest and fastest of its time. It reached speeds of 50 miles per hour. In the beginning of its run, passengers traveled up a long, slow hill, listening to the clicking of the tracks and the creaking of the wood. Then as they crested the hill, they felt their breaths taken away as their coaster took a 100-foot drop. Those swimming in the ocean could hear their collective screams—a regular sound on each trip of the coaster.

The Boulevard, once the railroad had moved its tracks inland, became a popular recreation area for Bostonians, as well as suburbanites. At one time it had four roller coasters. *Post card, circa 1920.*

If you came for excitement, the roller coasters could provide it, but they weren't the only fast moving, thrilling rides. In addition, the boulevard boasted "the Whip," the "Dodgems," the "Virginia Reel," "The Wild Mouse"—all fast-moving and exciting, as well as the tamer "Hippodrome," a merry-go-round with as many as five horses side by side in synchronized movement, more than any other ride in the world. Even the somewhat tame merry-go-rounds were called the "flying horses."

Do heights scare you more than speed? Well, then you might fancy the Ferris Wheel, or years later, a double wheel with a huge orbit. Closer to earth, but still stimulating, were a Fun House, and the scary "Bluebeard's Castle." And of course there were plenty of places to eat. One of the most famous and longest lasting is Kelly's Roast Beef, which shows up in all the guidebooks and still prospers today.

The beach resort hit its high during the 1930s and 1940s, when huge crowds appeared on many a sunny weekend or holiday afternoon. A large proportion of these crowds arrived by public transportation. Transit ran beneath Boston Harbor

A view of Revere Beach and the Boulevard, looking south, as it once looked. After a blizzard leveled many of the beach's structures, and the attractions had lost their allure, developers built high rise apartment buildings to capitalize on the fine views of the Atlantic. *Postcard, 1914.*

via the East Boston Tunnel to Maverick Square Station in East Boston, and trolleys took them from there to two points on Revere Beach: Beach Street or Revere Street. As these trolleys emptied, the Boulevard was awash with people.

During the Second World War, the beach was a favorite place for sailors and other servicemen. Revere gave its own sons and daughters to the war effort as well. In a strange bit of irony, some of those who were stationed on the island of Oahu, in Hawaii, thought they sensed something familiar about the train cars that took them to their barracks and around the island. Their senses served them well. It turned out that these cars had been sold by the Narrow Gauge Railroad when it was finally torn down.

Use of the beach declined from the 1950s on, and the blizzard of 1978 took a destructive toll on many of the buildings, most of which were by then no longer being used. However, in the 1980s, there was a renewal project. This included the building of high-rise condominiums and apartments, even office buildings. The old "Revere Beach" was gone. However, the same period saw the restoration of the boulevard, the pavilions, and the beach itself. In 2004, Revere Beach was listed as a National Historic Landmark.

⚓

Rumney Marsh and the Blue Line

Revere is more than just its famous beach. It has a recorded history that goes back to its first-known inhabitants, the Rumney Marsh Indians. We say these people were "inhabitants" because they weren't quite residents. They were more like summer visitors who came to the seashore during the warm weather, mostly to fish. They were also known to hold athletic contests on the beaches. Prizes were placed upon poles and the young men would compete for them. So beach volleyball may be fairly recent, but the idea to hold athletic games on beaches is not.

The 600 square acres of Rumney Marsh extend from Saugus in the north, southeast to Winthrop and were discovered by the omnipresent John Smith, when he explored the coast in 1614. The first person to live on the salt marsh was Samuel Maverick, in 1624. He lived at Winnisemmet, which is now called "Chelsea." The salt marsh was annexed to Boston along with what later became Chelsea and Winthrop. In 1641, a county road was built through the marsh to Salem. During King Phillip's War, the Indians, though friendly, were moved to Deer Island, where many died. After that, the remnants of the tribe mixed in with the English settlers.

In 1881, a part of Revere, called Point of Pines, became a summer resort with improved roads and lighting by natural gas. Following the summer vacation season, sportsmen used the area for duck hunting, and a tavern was built there for refreshments.

Revere became a city in 1915, and grew in population through the two wars, with many veterans who had visited there coming back to build houses, particularly under the post-World War II G.I. Bill.

Today, the town is mostly residential, a suburb of Boston, connected by commuter rail and the MBTA's Blue Line, which still uses the East Boston Tunnel.

Public transportation's Blue Line runs to Boston from Wonderland Station, much of the line along the right of way of the old Narrow Gauge tracks and the East Boston tunnel. This trolley is from an earlier time. *Postcard, 1906.*

⚓

Saugus

IRON, ICE, INDUSTRY

Saugus, settled first in 1629, was given the name from an Indian word that meant "extended" or "great." The town we now know as Saugus had been part of a much larger area called "Lin," or "Lynn." This territory included today's Lynn, Lynnfield, Nahant, Swampscott, Reading, and Wakefield. The town of Saugus was separated from Lynn and became a district in 1815.

Though most of its settlers were farmers, a significant industry began on the Saugus River in 1646. While the Saugus Iron Works lasted only twenty-two years, it was the first integrated iron works in North America. It ran until 1668.

The export and sale of ice began in Saugus when Frederick Tudor harvested (or cut) the ice from a pond on his family farm, insulated it with hay, took it to a dock (Tudor Wharf) in Charlestown, and shipped it to the tropics, mainly the Caribbean island of Martinique 1,500 miles away. His ship sailed away on February 10, 1806, and prompted a story in the *Boston Gazette*, that reported:

> No joke. A vessel has cleared at the Custom House for Martinique with a cargo of ice. We hope this will not prove a slippery speculation.

At first, that's all it was. Tudor lost heavily during his first years of operation, posting his first profit in 1810. Moreover, he generally lost money and spent time in debtors' prison. But Tudor was nothing if not tenacious. He continued to borrow money, make improvements, and try new ventures, like importing fruit from Cuba to New York, which he did in 1816. He borrowed $3,000, at the extravagant rate of forty percent interest, and buried oranges, limes, pears, and bananas in fifteen tons of ice and three tons of hay. All that insulation was not enough, though. Nearly all the fruit rotted and Tudor's fortunes soured as well. Still, he did not quit. He now shipped his ice to American warm-weather cities, including Charleston, Savannah, and New Orleans.

Tudor tried new kinds of insulation, like wood shavings, sawdust, and the chaff from rice, while stacking his blocks of ice together like bricks to reduce surface exposure, and he built icehouses in tropical locations while stirring up a demand for cold drinks. But it was new inventions that kept him and his ice afloat. Railroads made it easier to ship ice south to jumping-off points using insulated freight cars. Nathaniel Wyeth invented an ice saw, pulled by horses, to make ice cutting easier and faster. Tudor now tripled his production.

At this point, in 1833, he went into partnership with Sam Austin, a merchant from Boston. They shipped ice to India, a voyage of four months, on which they carried 180 tons of ice. The people in Calcutta thought it was some kind of joke, but 100 tons of the ice remained frozen, and Tudor made over $200,000 on his voyages to India. By the 1840s, ice was being shipped around the world, with many purveyors besides Tudor. He paid off his debts and lived comfortably, building a large house at the corner of Beacon and Joy Streets, near the State House.

The Industrial Revolution came to Massachusetts around 1830, and brought new industries like shoemaking and woolens to Saugus, while tobacco products were manufactured in the eastern part of town.

During this period, Saugus built its first town hall. That's not unusual, but the way they funded it is remarkable. The administration of U.S. President Andrew Jackson had actually managed to earn a surplus in its budget, paying off the national debt for the only time before or since. Congress decided to distribute the money to the states, and Saugus was a beneficiary, using $2,000 of it to build the town hall. Inflation, however, ensued, and when Saugus built its current town hall in 1837, it put the town $50,000 in debt.

This kind of debt, though it seems trifling to today's reader, was enough to spur East Saugus to try to join Lynn instead. However, its citizens weren't able to get their bill passed by both branches of the state legislature. Saugus politicians did what they have often done in such cases—they threw a bone to the petitioners and voted to spend $5,000 to lay water pipes through East Saugus as an appeasement—thus adding to the debt.

Saugus was situated favorably for transportation, lying on the route between Boston and Newburyport. About four miles of 1805's Newburyport Turnpike were built through the town, a span which is now U.S. Route 1. Thus, when the automobile came along, Saugus was ready, and an increase in traffic led to the widening of the road and to building an overpass in 1935 at Main Street. During the 1950s, many of the businesses you see today sprang up along the road. They brought substantial income to Saugus.

The railroad, with its passenger trains, ran through Saugus with the Eastern, Boston and Maine, and Grand Junction Railroad. Saugus had three depots. It also had recreation in the form of harness racing at the Franklin Trotting Park, known as Saugus Race Course. It had a hotel and a grandstand, and thousands of customers, until locals complained about the nature of these customers. They were not the kind of people wanted in Saugus, and the track was closed. The large, open space was used for a time for fairs, circuses, and auto racing, but in 1912, it became an airfield, the first to deliver airmail in New England, which lasted into the 1920s. Various proposals for use of the open space led to nothing, and in 1990 it was ceded to the Metropolitan District Commission (MDC).

Saugus has more than thirty lobster fishing boats, supposedly the largest number in the state. The town has a pier where they tie up, called, appropriately, Lobsterman's Landing. Not all of the boats landed there are from Saugus. Some commercial shellfishing also takes place in town. Clam beds are conditionally restricted and the clams must be purified in Newburyport before going to market.

Saugus can also claim to be home to the oldest barber shop in the country. George's Barber Shop in Cliftondale is more than 100 years old. The town also built the first successful incineration plant in 1975. It is still running.

⚓

East Boston

WHERE THE WHEELS TOUCH DOWN

East Boston's history has long been involved with transportation concerns. It was originally an area made up of six islands, Noddle, Hogg Breed's, Governor's, Bird, and Apple (Bird, once an island, was reduced to a shoal.) The largest, Noddle's Island, had been used to graze cattle and other animals, and during the Revolution, was the location of a battle for those livestock that became known as "The Battle of Chelsea Creek." It was the first naval engagement of that war.

After the Revolution, and long before the railroads came to East Boston, William H. Sumner (son of a Governor Increase Sumner) tried to have a highway built between Boston and Salem that would run in a straight line through East Boston, arguing that:

> the circular route from Chelsea thro' Charlestown to Boston is about 1 [*sic*] of a mile farther than a direct course over Noddle's Island in Boston.... The course suggested will be almost in a direct line, from my knowledge of the land.... On the back part of the Island is a muddy creek and the distance of the Island to Boston is not so great by one third, I presume as it is from Chelsea to Moreton Point in Charlestown.... There is no doubt then but that the necessities of the town of Boston will some require a connection with Noddle's Island with the town of which it is part.

A man in Sumner's position had to know, however, that a new U.S. navy yard was to be built in Charlestown (1801), and the bridge that would be required to link Boston and East Boston would be in the way of ships sailing into the harbor, so the Charlestown-Chelsea route was chosen instead. That did not, though, end the attempt to connect East Boston to the rest of Massachusetts by means of transportation.

William Sumner had a lot to do with the early growth of that area. Little by little, he bought up most of Noddle's Island. Then he and his partners formed the East Boston Company. Their plan was to sell shares in the island, but they needed to have a transportation link with Boston and other towns.

The East Boston Company wanted to establish a railroad between Boston and Salem and a ferry to Boston. Sumner soon owned much of Noddle's island real estate, and it would be worth nothing if no one could reach it. So transportation was a key to East Boston in the early days, and it remains so today. Geography was and is a key to history.

The company tried to convince the Eastern Railroad to come to East Boston, and did attract two ferries that ran from Lewis Wharf in Boston. A bridge was built between East Boston and Chelsea. Meanwhile, within East Boston, streets were laid out and houses built, mostly in support of the new East Boston Lumber Company, and the Boston Sugar Refinery, built in East Boston to make white granulated sugar.

Marshland was filled in, and by the middle of the 19th century, immigrants and other new residents began to arrive. Canadians and Irish came, among them P.J. Kennedy, who ran a tavern and was grandfather to U.S. President John F. Kennedy. Russian Jews and Italians settled in large numbers on Orient Heights. Later, there would be large numbers of families from Southeast Asia, and in recent decades, many Latin Americans settled around Maverick Square.

Transportation continued to be a central theme. With lumber came shipbuilding, and in Donald McKay's shipyard in mid-century, many of the

Closer to its downtown than most major airports, Logan Airport also has salt water on three sides. Takeoffs and landings are quite visible from points in Boston and Winthrop.

famous "clipper ships" were built and used in the China trade. These were the world's fastest ships in their day. His ships were built sleekly so that they could cut through the waves. Vessels like the *Flying Cloud* filled the sky with acres of sail. They carried cargo and passengers across the ocean in record times and brought many mariners and shipbuilders to East Boston.

Clipper ships also took part in the Gold Rush in California, when prospective miners rode them around the tip of South America in their hurry to be first to get to the gold fields. In fact, the *Flying Cloud* made the 1,600 mile voyage from Boston to San Francisco via Cape Horn in just ninety days—half the time taken by the previous record-holder. McKay's ships also took passengers to Australia in the hunt for gold a few years later.

East Boston and McKay's shipyard used the latest in the technology, including the first derrick in the Boston area, which lifted heavy timbers into place. McKay is gone, but not forgotten. An obelisk stands in his honor on Castle Island, while across the harbor, at Piers Park on Marginal Street in East Boston, there is a memorial to him. His house still stands on Eagle Hill on White Street.

The town was annexed by Boston in 1836. Ships were big on the East Boston waterfront in mid-century, but by 1904, the East Boston Tunnel opened as the first underwater tunnel of its kind in the country. It gave East Boston a connection with Boston via subway, while the Narrow Gauge Railroad gave it a connection with towns to the north.

An airfield, built on Jeffries Point in the 1920s, gradually expanded to become Logan Airport, one of the busiest airports in the U.S., but at great expense to the population, since many houses, especially on Neptune Road, were removed, and noise has been a continual complaint.

Logan Airport is closer to Boston than most other airports are to their cities, and has unique landing approaches over the ocean and harbor islands. Many visitors say they hadn't realized they were about to land until they actually felt the wheels touch down. There has, however, been tension between East Boston (and Winthrop) residents and companies that run the airport. In one expansion, the area called Wood Island Park, designed by famed landscape architect Frederick Law Olmsted, was taken. Each subsequent expansion has brought conflict.

More houses were taken to build the Sumner Tunnel, named for the developer, in 1934. Two other vehicular tunnels followed, the Callahan, in 1961, and the Ted Williams Tunnel, in 1995, which allow passengers to reach the airport more quickly from downtown and the south, while bypassing most of East Boston.

⚓

Winthrop

NORTHERN GATEWAY TO BOSTON HARBOR

Another community developed by the railroad was Winthrop. The town of Winthrop occupies a curving peninsula that helps to enclose Boston Harbor as a protected inlet from the Atlantic Ocean. Its, long, curving finger nearly "shakes hands" with Long Island to the south in providing a barrier. The town has views of Boston to the west, or inside of the peninsula, and views of the ocean to the east or outside. On the north, it connects with East Boston and Revere.

The native Massachusetts tribe called the area that contains Winthrop and these surrounding towns and cities "Winnisimmet." Winthrop, called Pullen Poynt, had little known history during the first years of colonial settlement of the North Shore area, but was annexed by Boston in 1632, and during the first five of those years was used mainly to graze farm animals from those who lived in Boston.

At the end of that "grazing period," land here was parceled out into fifteen sections to friends of Massachusetts Governor Winthrop—mainly those who were most prominent in Boston. They had to promise, however, to erect a building on their new holdings within two years. Though these men kept and tended farms on the peninsula, few, if any of them, lived here.

One of the earliest houses, built during the first half of the 1600s and rebuilt in 1675, was the home of Deane Winthrop, the governor's youngest son. He lived in it until his death in 1703, and it is for him that the town is named. The house remains and is cared for by the Winthrop Improvement and Historical Association.

The areas of Winthrop, Revere, and Chelsea withdrew from Boston in 1739, and these eventually became separate entities, Winthrop becoming a town in 1752. The town is on a peninsula with seven miles of coastline.

It is also connected by causeway to Deer Island in Shirley Gut. The island is named for the deer who swam over from the mainland when threatened by wolves. Deer Island has a significant history, not all of it admirable. It was used as an internment camp for Native Americans during King Phillip's War, as a quarantine station for immigrants, many of whom died, as a county jail for petty criminals, a reform school for juvenile delinquents, an orphanage, and a military post. It presently houses the huge Deer Island Waste Water Treatment Plant, a sewage-treatment plant for forty-three communities in the Boston area, keeping Boston Harbor one of the cleanest in any metropolitan area.

In 1775, Winthrop colonists joined those from other area towns and American militia in the Battle of Chelsea Creek (described in detail in the chapter of the same name).

The neighborhoods today include Court Park and Cottage Park along the Boston Harbor side of town, Point Shirley and Cottage Hill on either side of what was Shirley Gut, and Winthrop Beach, Ocean Spray, and Winthrop Heights on the Massachusetts Bay side.

Visitors and residents to Winthrop enjoy its seven miles of seacoast and spectacular views of Boston. It has much to offer within a small area.

⚓

Battle of Chelsea Creek

During the Revolutionary War, colonists managed to pen the British up in the port of Boston with their backs to the sea. Even though the vaunted British army and its navy—long the best in the world—had superior fire power and better trained units, the colonists had superior numbers and had dug in so efficiently that any British attempt at a break out would meet punishing resistance.

However, the sea door remained open and that's how supplies were arriving from England and from Nova Scotia, or the West Indies. The British, nonetheless, had shortfalls in some areas. One of them was fodder for the cavalry's horses, and they had already attempted to gather hay from Grape Island, in Weymouth, with limited success before being driven off by the locals who burned what the British weren't able to abscond with.

The British and the Patriots then both understood the game that was afoot and would scramble for the remaining resources from harbor islands and maritime shores. One such area was just north of Boston. Noddle's Island and Hog Island, today comprise much of the peninsula of East Boston—but not in those days. They also held no airport or airplanes, but they did hold both livestock and farm products, and so they were valuable and the British commander General Gage viewed them as a resource.

However, like much of the British movement in those pre-independence days, Gage's strategy was plodding and insufficient. The Patriots were like a professional sports team that is always beating their bigger opponents to the ball or the puck. They seemed always to have the British back on their heels, and this would be no different.

Clearly the islands of Hog and Noddle were well within the British sphere of influence and any Patriots trespassing thereupon would be tantamount to putting their heads in a hot oven. But the Patriots were up to such things, and the British were slow to react. The Patriots who farmed on those islands tended to be loyalist in their leanings, and anyway they had little choice. If they sold their produce to the British, as they usually did, then the Patriots had a word for them: "traitors." They would become harbor scum if ever the Patriots drove the British out of Boston.

Well, why not refuse to sell their goods to the British? Then the British army would simply take what they wanted and the farmers of the islands would become rebels in the eyes of the nearby British, who were used to helping themselves to whatever they wanted and needed.

But not so fast—or not so slow, for before the British could consolidate their hold on those needed livestock and grains, the fast-moving Patriots put their own oar into the water. On May 14, 1775, Joseph Warren, who headed the Massachusetts Committee of Safety, ordered that the livestock be taken by the Patriots from "... Noddle's Island, Hog Island, Snake Island, and that part of Chelsea near the sea coast...." The cattle and other beasts were to be removed to the safety of Patriot-held towns, like Medford, Malden, and Lynn.

Warren called for a force to be assigned to this task from the regiment that was now besieging Boston from Medford. Warren, you see, had a lot on the ball. He wasn't someone to let his opponents make the first move and then react to their foray. No, indeed; Brother Warren was an actor. He took a tour with General Artemus Ward, to see for himself the lay of the land in (what we would call) East Boston.

For those of you who already know the lay of the land, we can tell you that Hog Island was where Orient Heights is now, and Noddle's Island took up most of the remainder of East Boston. The reconnaissance trip was risky, but there were no British on either island at first, and, although the owners of the cattle and hogs had moved most of their herds away from the coast to the centers of the islands, there were some stragglers who could easily be taken. The Patriots went after those.

General Ward named Col. John Stark of New Hampshire, who would later be a hero at Bunker Hill, to handle this job. He would be a good choice. For one thing, he was stationed nearby, at Somerville's Winter Hill just away from the isthmus that led from Charlestown to Somerville, and closer still to the bridge across the Mystic River that led to Medford. Stark had 300 of his own New Hampshire men, plus others from towns around Boston.

On May 27th, three weeks before the Battle of Bunker Hill, Stark's men crossed into Medford just after midnight. They headed north through Malden, and what are now Everett and Revere. The tread of their marching drew attention and adherents, so the longer they marched, the larger their force became.

As they got near to Hog Island, scouts reported that the British had left about fifty marines after Warren and Ward had looked the place over. Stark sent some men across the shallow water of Belle Isle Marsh. By that time, it was mid-morning and these men set about rounding up livestock at Stark's order. He also led thirty men across Crooked Creek to Noddle's Island, where they broke into groups and busied themselves slaughtering animals, so that the British couldn't have them and setting fire to crops and barns. The fires, however, attracted attention from the Royal Marines who were quartered on that island, and they attacked, scattering the Patriots.

The smoke was also seen by Admiral Graves from his flagship in the harbor, and he sent additional marines, raising their numbers to about 400. They pushed Stark's smaller band toward Crooked Creek, but its tall grass allowed the Patriots to set up a line of defense and begin a pitched battle that lasted late into the afternoon. The Patriots suffered only three casualties.

This now looked serious to Graves, so he sent the schooner *Diana* up Chelsea Creek, on the west side of Noddle's and Hog's Islands, as well as

The little-known skirmish with the British took place in the waters around East Boston, Revere, and Chelsea, many known by earlier names. *Taken from an actual survey. Humbly inscribed to "Richd. Whitworth by J. De Costa; C. Hall, sc." Hand-colored map 37 X 49 cm. Created: July 29 1775.*

the tender from HMS *Somerset*, a small ship named *Brittania*. The *Diana* should have provided just the kind of opposition that the British were capable of. It was 120 tons, fairly new, and it had four six-pounder cannons, as well as a dozen swivel guns. Graves's nephews commanded both of these ships.

Also available for the British counterattack were eight barges of Royal Marines, who meant to get behind Stark so that he could not retreat from the islands. *Diana* also meant to move behind Stark's men, so it sailed north in Chelsea Creek. But by the time it got there and its crew trained their guns on the island, the Royal Marines on the island had retreated into the interior, and Stark's men, no longer under intense fire, had evacuated Noddle's Island for Hog's Island, where Stark had most of his men.

The cat and mouse game continued. The British ships headed further up the creek, always just behind their prey. By sunset, the Patriots had driven hundreds of cattle, horses, and hogs off Hog Island and onto the mainland (now called "Revere" after the Patriot leader), and out of range, while some of their number kept a covering fire on the British marines, so they were unable to land on the mainland.

Stark's men stood in brackish water higher than their waists, firing on the two ships. This was more than the British could bear. These damned rebels had been in their face once too often, and the *Diana* and *Britannia* sailed into the shallow waters to finish them off. This was unwise. British seamen ought to have known better than to sail into shallow water where they had no idea of the depth, but they let their emotions get the better of their judgments.

Mother Nature was not with Mother Britain. With just under an hour of daylight left, the winds shifted and so did the river current, and the schooner and sloop both ran aground in the muddy bottom of the marshy Chelsea Creek. The men in the barges tied ropes to both ships and tried to tow them free.

But this was a full-attention task. The marines couldn't tow the ships and fire at the rebels, too, so they lowered their heads and pulled with a will. That led the Patriots to turn the tide and fire on the British marines.

This would be short-lived, however. The sailors got their boats attached by line to the larger vessels and managed to get them both downstream to the southwest where the water was deeper, and where they were far enough from the Patriots to be out of range. They then headed west across the creek to the Winnisimmet side (now Chelsea), just at the mouth of the creek where it met the Mystic River.

The major force of the Patriots was busy doing scrambling of its own. They headed around to the north and west side of the creek and made it to Winnisimmet in time to meet the arriving British ships and fire on them from shore. Not only that, but reinforcements under the dynamic and fearless General Israel Putnam were on their way, and by 9 p.m., 300 of them emerged from the darkness with two cannons. The fire from shore was so withering that the rowers had to allow the *Diana* to drift while they saved themselves.

The wind and current came to the fore a second time and *Diana* floated south to the shore of the Mystic River in Chelsea and became grounded once again. The *Britannia* met a better fate since those towing it were able to get it into deep water.

The tide was going out, and that made *Diana's* position steadily worse. The irrepressible Putnam waded out into the waist-deep water and hailed the *Diana*, telling its crew that they must give up the ship and, if they did, he would treat them fairly. They refused. Finally the schooner listed to one side, even as its crew continued to fire its cannon while sliding down the decks as they tried to stay upright. At the last they jumped into the water and swam to the *Britannia*.

When that ship had sailed away with the crews of both vessels, the Patriots boarded the empty schooner and picked it clean, gathering things their side sorely needed, including iron, guns, sails, rope, and even cash. Then they took some of that hay they had gathered and stuffed it into the dry parts of the boat and set it on fire. The bonfire was easily seen in Boston and by the surrounding troops, signaling an colonial victory and the capture of a British ship by the green but energetic colonials.

Summary

The North Shore has seen some of the country's most colorful and curious history and remains a vibrant area where many people choose to live. This account gives you an overview of this history and some depth on certain people and events. It has been said that all history is local, and if you piece together the various stories from the different towns and places, you will have a good view of the area's history and even that of the whole United States. Somehow coastal areas produce fascinating stories—which we choose to call "Lore." We can hope that the places and stories have been so alluring that you will wish to visit some or all of them soon.

Bibliography

Books

Baker, Bob. *Two Days for Ever from Marblehead Celebrates 350 Years of Democracy 1649-1999*. Marblehead 350th Anniversary of Incorporation Committee, 1999.

Cheney, Charles Edward. *The Barefoot Maid at the Fountain Inn*. Chicago, IL: Chicago Literary Club, 1911.

Clarke, Ted. *Boston Curiosities*. Charleston, SC: The History Press, 2007.

Clarke, Ted. *Thomas Watson: Does That Name Ring a Bell?* Parker: CO:Outskirts Press, 2006.

Donald A. Doliber. *The First Inhabitants of Marblehead from Marblehead Celebrates 350 Years of Democracy 1649-1999*. Marblehead 350th Anniversary of Incorporation Committee, 1999.

History of USM: 1899-1905. Beverly, MA: Beverly Historical Society, 2000.

Hoisington, Daniel J. *Made in Beverly: A History of Beverly Industry*. Beverly Historic District Commission, 1989.

Lord, Priscilla Sawyer and Virginia Clegg Gamage. *Marblehead—The Spirit of '76 Lives Here*, Chilton Book Company, 1972.

Mitchell, Barbara. *Shoes for Everyone: A Story About Jan Matzeliger*. Minneapolis, MN: Carolrhoda Books, 1986.

Electronic Sources

"1860 Showmakers Strike in Lynn" Massachusetts AFL-CIO. www.massaflcio.org/1860-showmakers-strike-lynn.

Account of Leslie's Retreat at the North Bridge in Salem, on Sunday, February 26,1775. http://www.archive.org/stream/accountofleslies00endi/accountofleslies00endi_djvu.txt.

Battle of Chelsea Creek. http://totallyhistory.com/battle-of-chelsea-creek.

Boston, Revere Beach & Lynn Railroad, by Francis B. C. Bradleem (1921). http://www.celebrateboston.com/mbta/brbl-history.htm

Bradlee, Francis B. "Boston, Revere Beach * Lynn Railroad. http://www.celebrateboston.com/mbta/brbl-history.htm.

Chidsey, Donald Barr. The American Privateers. http://penelope.uchicago.edu/Thayer/E/Gazetteer/Places/America/United_States/_Topics/history/_Texts/CHITAP/18*.html.

D'Entremont, Jeremy. "The Lost Light of Egg Rock." Lighthouse Digest.www.lhdigest.com/digest/StoryPage.cfm?StoryKey=421

"East Boston, Suffolk County, MA." Suffolk County Gen Web. http://suffolkctymagenweb.org/eastboston.html

Friends of Lynn Woods: Dungeon Rock. http://www.flw.org/dungeonrockhistory.htm.

Hawthorne, Nathaniel, "Browne's Folly." 1860. http://www.eldritchpress.org/nh/brnf.html.

LaMontagne, Kori. "The Economic Impact on the Evolution of the Landscape of Beverly from the Post-Revolutionary Period to 1920." PrimaryResearch.org, 2013.